The Power
of You

ABOUT THE AUTHOR

Anne Jones is a gifted and experienced healer who has helped many people understand themselves, heal scars of trauma, reclaim their confidence and improve their self-esteem. Anne spends her time giving workshops and retreats, making guest appearances on TV and radio and touring the world with her work. She is also the founder of Ripple UK Ltd and Hearts and Hands for Africa – a registered charity which is supported by the profits raised from all of her work.

Anne is the author of six books for Piatkus: *Heal Yourself*, *Healing Negative Energy*, *The Ripple Effect*, *Opening Your Heart* and *The Soul Connection*.

The Power of You

SIMPLE STEPS TO DEVELOP
YOUR INNER STRENGTH,
MASTER YOUR FEARS AND
LIVE TO YOUR GREATEST
POTENTIAL

Anne Jones

piatkus

PIATKUS

First published in Great Britain in 2011 by Piatkus

A CIP catalogue record for this book
is available from the British Library.

ISBN 978-0-7499-5399-7

Typeset in Bembo by Palimpsest Book Production Ltd, Falkirk, Stirlingshire
Printed and bound in Great Britain by the MPG Books Group, Bodmin, Cornwall

Papers used by Piatkus are natural, renewable and recyclable
products sourced from well-managed forests and certified
in accordance with the rules of the Forest Stewardship Council.

Mixed Sources
Product group from well-managed
forests and other controlled sources
www.fsc.org Cert no. SGS-COC-004081
© 1996 Forest Stewardship Council
FSC

Piatkus
An imprint of
Little, Brown Book Group
100 Victoria Embankment
London EC4Y 0DY

An Hachette UK Company
www.hachette.co.uk

www.piatkus.co.uk

CONTENTS

To Tone, who has struggled through the worst nightmares and fought his demons with determination. Bless you Tony, and thank you for inspiring this book.

And to Mousie, my dear mother, who has recovered her health through determination to gain a measure of independence and shows me daily the true power of fortitude, stoicism and fighting spirit. Her generation did not use up all their reserves of endurance and courage in the war – they can still show us the way!

ACKNOWLEDGEMENTS

A big thank you to Gill Bailey for her timely phone call to allow me to put my passionate feelings about this subject into print.

A huge thank you to Rebecca Woods for her tremendous work as editor. Her professional input and her care and insights have been supportive and invaluable.

Thanks to Tanya for sitting beside me while I pounded on the keys, giving constant companionship and inspiration, only interrupting when nature called. You will always be remembered, sweetheart.

A huge thank you to Kaia, not only for her comments on the environment but also for creating a beautiful logo to represent the Power of You.

Thank you to Debbie who has listened to my ideas, endured my rantings when I discovered yet another case of injustice and inspired me throughout.

And as always, bless you, Brenda and Tony, for your full-on support and love – I couldn't do any of this without you.

INTRODUCTION

Within each of us we hold a core essence of kindness, sympathy, compassion, strength, fortitude and courage. We have a will that springs from the very core of our being to create, to fulfil dreams, to help others, to improve and grow. This will is quite unique to humankind – it is our personal power. It is the purest form of human spirit, and although it may be damaged, hidden or disabled, it is our true essence. This is the very precious aspect of ourselves that I want to help you rediscover, develop and bring into action, so that your life can be richer in every way and you can live your life to its fullest and most magnificent potential.

'When empowered you can expand beyond the limitations of your mind.'

Aspects of this power come forward at different times of our lives: as strength and courage when we face danger; as fortitude when we are pushed to our limit; as joy when something magnificent occurs, like the birth of a baby. When our power is activated and in full force we are able to fulfil our greatest potential in every respect at all times, not just when we face extreme situations. This activation is empowerment and with empowerment comes enthusiasm and passion for life. It brings forth all those vital and positive aspects of our human spirit, so that no task or challenge seems impossible. This enables us to step beyond the limits of self-doubt and move through our fears. We can find happiness and joy through the fulfilment of living our lives to their fullest.

I am writing this book with passion and urgency as my contribution to assisting us to reclaim our personal power. Through my work as a healer I see how many of us battle our individual fears and the factors that limit us. We may struggle with anger, judgement and intolerance, but these are behaviour and attitudes adopted to cope with emotional pain and low self-esteem. When we discard the negative outer coat, we find the pure gold of our true spirit inside.

I have also become conscious of a growing level of fear that permeates all levels of society and virtually every country in the world today. This fear unsettles and disempowers individuals, who in turn adversely affect families and thereby communities and nations. In other words, we are all affected by the negative forces that flow around us. In my own family I have come face to face with the devastating effects of this negativity and fear, so I have an intense personal interest in offering and sharing solutions that I have found to be effective.

When you are disempowered you are prey to self-doubt, to bullies and fears. You are susceptible to negative forces, whether they come from your own mind, from other individuals or from corporations and governments. You lose your faith in your sense of spirit, the safety of the world in which you live and your ability to support yourself and others.

How do you know if you are not living your life fully in your power? Here are a few indicators:

✧ You are not motivated or passionate about your work.

✧ You 'can't be bothered'.

✧ Your illness record at work is poor.

✧ You find it difficult to raise your game.

✧ You find enthusiastic and upbeat people irritating.

✧ You find it difficult to get out of bed in the morning.

✧ You feel depressed, uninspired, confused or miserable.

✧ You are dominated, suppressed or even bullied by other people.

✧ You don't think you are good enough.

✧ You live with anxiety.

✧ You are unable to express your feelings.

✧ You are overwhelmed by the negativity in the media.

✧ You feel hopeless and helpless to change either your life or the world.

✧ You get easily dispirited, giving up and giving in are the easy options.

✧ You find it difficult to complete any task or reach any goal.

✧ You live in fear: fear of loss of free will and ability to choose, of ill health, of attack, of loss of status, of loss of possessions, of failure, of inability to provide for your family, of dependency on family or state, of addiction.

All of these states of being take you away from your true state of self, which is strength, independence, joy, love and harmony.

Through my own journey of healing I have been able to connect to my inner strength and core energy. This has allowed me to run a healing organisation and a charity, to write books and to travel extensively giving seminars and public appearances – all of which need a deep well of energy. However, I have also experienced how it feels when the connection slips away. Last year I went through a complete fallout. My stepson had suffered a mental breakdown and was hospitalised, while my mother had a stroke that left her traumatised and wheelchair-bound. I became overwhelmed by my anxieties. I lost my courage and strength as I struggled to support my family, cope with the shock and emotional strain and continue with my work. I felt torn in two. I felt weak and my heart raced. I experienced full-blown panic attacks and the fear immobilised me, I literally froze in anxiety.

After several restless, sleepless nights and discordant, panicky days I went into my garden one day, found a seat, closed my eyes and asked for help and guidance. Immediately I realised that I had allowed myself to fall into fear. I was looking at every problem and every situation through the eyes of fear. I was not walking my own talk. So I meditated – I used a visualisation, a guided meditation that I have used with my clients many times – and took myself back into my heart centre, which is where we create and experience love. Instantly, I felt better. I felt myself getting stronger and more at peace. My heart grew calm and my thoughts rational. I could then see there were options that I hadn't even considered, and within two days these had been put forward to the family and solutions began to fall into place. Once again I had realised that love is the key; we can find clarity and harmony when we focus on our problems from the perspective of love.

In this book my intention is to look at the many challenges that we face daily, challenges that can diminish and deplete our power and true sense of self, and show how we can reclaim and protect our extraordinary inner energy force. I will help you to counter, modify, heal and clear your negativity and assist you to withstand the forces that challenge and diminish your inner power. With exercises, meditations and opportunities to look deep within, I will show you how you can find the joy that is the essential spirit of everyone, even though sometimes it may be hidden beneath many layers of spiritual and emotional pain.

These changes we make for ourselves have a wider implication. As many of us hold the intention to change and work on ourselves and take responsibility for the state of our environment and planet, so they will improve too. Each small, positive action and change of attitude towards ourselves; every time we step through our limitations; every act of kindness towards ourselves, other people and our environment – they all make a difference. They ripple out and change the world, so that the mass consciousness of our combined thoughts and feelings improves and becomes lighter, more positive and more joyful, and every individual benefits.

'The future of the world is in our positive intentions and personal acts of hope, kindness and love.'

We live in a world that is changing fast. I truly believe that the long-term outcomes of these changes will be positive. But, as we work through the chaos that they create, we need all the help we can get to maintain our inner and personal strength and harmony. I hope you find my contribution helps you to regain and restore your own sense of personal power and control, so that you can see your life through the perspective of strength and self-determination.

I have written the book as a guide that you can read

through from cover to cover, dip into intuitively or use for reference. The exercises and meditations are recorded on a CD which you can order from my website (see appendix).

START A JOURNAL

Throughout this book I will be sharing exercises that may include writing your own feelings and thoughts on a given subject, so I suggest you get a notebook that can act as your journal. You can then add any inspirations or thoughts that come to you – as you record them, you anchor the energy more fully. Give your journal a title that holds your intention.

ONE

Developing Your Personal Power

You can live your life with a sense of fulfilment. You can feel strong and confident. You can speak up when you see injustice. You can do everything with your greatest ability. You can live without fear and with courage. You can live joyfully. You can do all this and more when you are empowered.

To begin, let us look at the personal power that I believe we all have. What is it? How can it be defined? What does it mean to you? I will then take you through the many aspects of your power and show ways you can encourage, uplift and develop them.

WHAT IS YOUR PERSONAL POWER?

Your personal power is the fullest and most powerful expression of your true self. This means that you don't have to aspire to be somebody else or to change into something else. You just need to allow your true self to shine, strong and uninhibited. We all have a core essence that is the same and we all have individual traits that are unique to each one of us. As we progress through this book I will give you opportunities to focus on your own strengths and skills, as well as exercises to empower and bring these to the fore. Here let's look at the basic elements that we all have – *every single one of us* – that together, when they are fully functional and unfettered, give us our personal power. The following list came directly from a workshop I held and includes the words that the attendees used to describe the various elements that they believed make up this power. Write them down in your journal and add any suggestions of your own:

Confidence	Self-worth	Conviction
Love	Self-responsibility	Determination
Inner wisdom	Awareness	Self-acceptance
Flexibility	Gratitude	The truth
Choice	Self-belief	Self-reliance
In control	Balance	Radiance
Understanding	Trust	Joy
Creator	Happiness	Strong voice
Independence	Strength	Focus
Resilience	Courage	

And probably the most powerful of all . . . Will.

LIVING WITH YOUR INNER POWER

To give you an idea what can come from living with your power fully recovered and operational, you may find it helpful to look at others who have managed to find theirs. You may have friends, colleagues or acquaintances who live their lives this way. How do you identify them? Let me give you some ideas:

✧ They look for the positive in everything they do and in every situation. If things take a downturn they ride it out and are always looking for the upturn. They live constantly with their cup half full rather than half empty.

✧ They give off a positive radiance and will light up a room when they enter, uplifting everyone around them.

✧ They see obstacles as something to challenge their wits and experience rather than as a sign that the world is turning against them. They do not retreat into fear when they are challenged.

✧ They go out of the box. They allow themselves to go beyond the limit of conventions and the influence of other people's limiting mindsets.

✧ They are courageous and able to stand out against the crowd if they feel committed. They are not constrained by expectations.

✧ They live with integrity and will do what they believe to be the right thing, even if it's challenged and a difficult or unpopular choice.

✧ They will be able to overcome physical adversity and find superhuman strength when needed.

✧ They live their life with passion and purpose – never with antipathy, lethargy or an 'I don't care' attitude.

✧ They take full responsibility for themselves and have a sense of shared responsibility for the wellbeing of friends, family and their community.

✧ They are focused and determined.

✧ They withstand criticism and the negative attitudes of individuals, organisations and the media.

✧ They are not afraid to express their feelings. For example, they are able to cry without embarrassment.

✧ They have a rubber-ball mentality, a durability that pulls them back up after disappointments and allows them to see failures as learning experiences.

✧ They hold respect and tolerance for themselves and others.

✧ They live from their hearts, loving and accepting themselves and others for who they are without criticism, understanding that everyone is on a different stage of their journey.

ICONS OF SELF-EMPOWERMENT

Let me name some well-known individuals and personal heroes of mine who are living and working in their power. They inspire me and give me courage when I am faced with challenges and when I am shooting for a goal that seems elusive. They all have one thing in common – the ability to go through their fears and do their best without being daunted by other people's opinions and criticism. Remember they have fears – everyone has – but they manage to overcome them and work through them and don't let them dominate or stultify their work or their lives.

Sir Richard Branson – businessman, entrepreneur and owner of Virgin Airlines. In business I use him as a role model. His upbeat approach and cheerful fearlessness makes him a popular figure and a likeable man. He has broken the stereotype of the grim-faced businessman, withdrawn from and above the people. I think of him when I get fearful and nervous facing a business decision. He shows me that it's OK to make mistakes, for he has made mistakes and had failures and yet keeps bobbing back up.

Karren Brady – formerly the youngest chief executive of a UK public company and the CEO of Birmingham City Football Club, flying the flag for empowered women and looking stunning as well. She has destroyed the perception of a glass ceiling in the business world for women by working in the man's world of football and taking on some of the world's greatest male egos. I also take inspiration from her as a speaker – she is honest and fun.

Nelson Mandela – statesman and world leader. He models forgiveness, courage and fortitude. He was imprisoned for years for his political beliefs yet he never gave up hope. When I feel that things are moving slowly and when I get discouraged, I think of him holding his vision alone in his cell year after year. He is a great and dignified man, proof that not all politicians are self-serving and corrupt.

Jonny Wilkinson – rugby player and scorer of the winning penalty at the World Cup in Sydney (I was there, Jonny). He has suffered terrible injuries but comes back again and again. As with many great sportsmen and women, it's his total dedication and giving of his all that is inspirational. I love and am inspired by people who give of themselves totally to whatever they do.

The Dalai Lama – spiritual leader, a positive angel and ambassador for Tibetan Buddhism. A man I dream of meeting, he has been persecuted and driven from his own country, yet continues to be a living example of humility and compassion. He walks his talk, and that's what I so admire. When you read about the disgrace and poor behaviour of many of our religious teachers, think of him, Gandhi and Mother Teresa, who all fully lived their beliefs.

All these people have lived their lives to their greatest potential. Many of them have faced huge opposition and almost insurmountable challenges, but still have held strong. They are great role models. Who are yours? Jot down their names in your journal and say why they inspire you. When you are feeling ineffective and undervalued, or when life has pushed you down, think of them and let them encourage you to dig deep and find your resilience. It's there under the fear of failure; have another go.

PHYSICAL AND MENTAL ENDURANCE

Although this personal power or human spirit is with us at all times, aspects of it can lie dormant until we face a particularly challenging, even dangerous time. Joe Simpson, a mountaineer, connected to his capacity for endurance and fortitude in an experience he describes in his book *Touching the Void*. He and his climbing partner, Simon Yates, were descending after a successful climb of the vertical face of the Siula Grande in Peru when disaster overcame them. Joe fell and broke his knee. Simon then had to lower him on ropes down the side of the mountain. He lowered Joe over a cliff overhang, but further disaster struck as they hit an impasse. Simon could not pull Joe up as his holding point was crumbling, while Joe couldn't climb up because of his broken leg. Unable either to see or hear Joe, and in a precarious position, Simon decided after much soul searching to cut the rope and hope that Joe had a soft landing. However, when Simon reached the crevice and peered over, he could neither see nor hear Joe. Presuming his partner had fallen to the bottom and perished, he had no choice but to continue his journey back to base camp.

Actually, Joe had fallen onto a ledge deep within the crevice. When he realised that Simon was not coming for him he managed to abseil down to the bottom and crawled out onto the glacier. For the next three days, without food or water, he crawled and hopped in intense agony over the most difficult terrain back to the base camp and arrived just as his colleagues were packing up to go home. This story of determination and endurance has gone down in mountaineering folklore, but for us it's an example of the depths that we can reach within ourselves when needed, and of the power of the human spirit to find resources of physical and mental strength and determination.

There are many stories of endurance and of individuals' ability to survive by drawing on inner forces. We need to connect to these depths of courage and strength, not just when we are in great danger or when disaster hits, but in our everyday lives. One outstanding feature of all my icons is their approach to fear − they do not let it limit them. They walk towards their fears rather than run from them. I am sure that every one of them has felt fear at some stage but they have not allowed negativity to destroy their dream. Joe Simpson could have become frozen by his fears. He could easily have given up at any stage of that journey − remember, he also had to cope with the emotional baggage of having been abandoned, for that was most definitely what he felt at the time. We will be taking a further look at how fear can sabotage our dreams in Chapter 2.

So, hopefully, you have managed to identify at least one person who inspires you with their ability to live from their personal power, and can act as a role model in your journey of self-empowerment.

INTENTIONS AND JOURNEYS

Whenever you are looking for change in your life you start with an intention. Intention is the force of your mind to give a focus to where you want to be, whether this be a goal at work, a life role change or a physical change, as in dieting or becoming more healthy. Any move forward to a different and hopefully a more positive state needs to be driven with an intention.

'With your intention set your journey begins.'

When you hold an intention to resolve some of your emotional issues you are choosing to change spiritually – a change which has become synonymous with a life journey. All around us there are people talking about their 'journey'. It is a useful analogy as it shows that once the intention is set, then you move forward. Journeys are often beset with difficulties, obstacles and setbacks, but from the very first step you will most definitely gain experience and knowledge which take you closer to your inner self and power.

'The journey that you are setting out on is the journey to discover, reclaim and defend your personal power.'

To give a journey purpose, you need a goal. I suggest that, in working through this book, you hold the intention to unleash your inner power. Know that this will give you the opportunity to live your life to its greatest potential.

Exercise: Stating your intention

In order to start your journey in any particular direction you need a goal. Think what your goal may be, then say it out loud and write it down in your journal – for example, 'My intention is to unleash my inner power and live my life to its greatest potential.' You can write down any of the items listed earlier in the chapter as a power list of the aspects of yourself you wish to reclaim. Whenever you feel down, weakened, frightened or overwhelmed, refer to your personal power list and know that every aspect is within you and belongs to you – they just need to be recovered. You can also use your journal to write down any other personal goals and healing you want to achieve.

THE HUMAN ENERGY FIELD

When our energy is strong we are strong in every way. We can stand up for ourselves, we are motivated and can fight off disease. In other words, when we are empowered we are strong in every way, because the energy of our thoughts and mind, the energy of our spirit and emotions and the energy of our body interconnect and impact each other. When we are empowered, positive vibrations flow through our energy field. Let's now see how this works.

Every cell of your body has its own micro energy field, and all the cells combined create a larger force field of energy. This greater energy field is called the aura, a Greek word meaning breeze, and it flows around the outside of the body for about three feet or more. Mostly it is invisible to the eye, although psychics can see the range of colours that it reflects. Most of us sense it through our intuition and sixth sense – that sense of knowing and experiencing that is called our gut feeling. The vibration, strength and brightness of this energy reflects your physical, mental and emotional well-being. If you are depressed and dispirited, feeling disempowered and overwhelmed, then it will seem dull and low. If you are happy, energised and full of life then your aura will be shining brightly, clear in colour and vibrant. In fact, when we say someone is vibrant we are referring to our sense of the vitality of their energy field. Your aura shifts

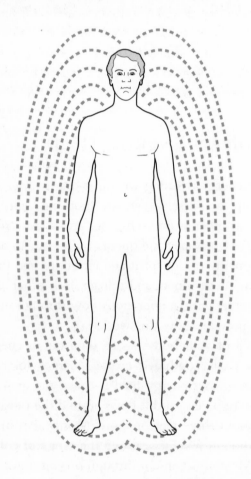

Aura – human energy field

and changes its vibrations as your mood swings and your thoughts change, reflecting your feelings and emotions through shape and colour.

Your aura is a beacon of energy, radiating out the mood you are in and affecting everyone close by. Similarly you are affected by the aura of everyone around you. As their auras radiate negative or positive energies, so these mix with your own energy and either bring your spirits and energy levels up or down. In the past, when I joined a group of people I would always feel a sort of butterfly sensation in my stomach similar to a fit of nerves, and for years I thought I was nervous of large groups. I now realise that other people's feelings affect me. You will probably have the same experience. For example, you will sense the positive and uplifting experience of celebration when joining a party of friends.

We monitor the vibrations of other people's energies through seven major centres or chakras (a Sanskrit word meaning wheel), spinning vortexes of energy that bring sensations and moods to and from internal and external sources. The state of these centres and the energies they monitor affect the life force energy that flows continuously through our body.

'Your positive feelings are energies that radiate out and affect everyone else.'

Our behaviour and the actions we take are governed by instinct from the actual energies these scanners pick up. The chakras are sending and receiving sensations all the time – sensations relating to our feelings and physical state, and those of the people around us. When you feel upset or disturbed, don't immediately blame yourself but understand it may be that you are affected by the feelings and thoughts of the people around you.

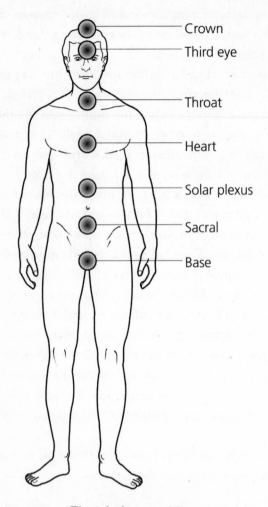

Crown

Third eye

Throat

Heart

Solar plexus

Sacral

Base

The chakra positions

THE SOLAR PLEXUS – THE KEY INFLUENCE TO PERSONAL POWER

This centre governs the energies of strength, will and self-esteem and is quick to pick up the fears and anxieties of others, as this is where you hold your own fears. The solar plexus is the chakra located just above the navel. Psychics using their inner vision see it as a yellow spinning force and by its name we see its connection to the sun's immense force of energy: *sol* is the Latin word for sun. In the past we acknowledged and revered the power of the sun and it was worshipped by many cultures including Africans, Japanese, Aztecs and Egyptians. This is hardly surprising, as the sun is by far the most naturally powerful force of energy in our universe and a visible source of the energy that nurtures our food chain. Although it's not necessary to submit to worship or create an icon of the sun, I recommend that you focus on its spiritual aspect, the spirit of the sun, which is called the Solar Logos. Through this spiritual connection you can access the universal energies of strength and power that the sun radiates and epitomises for us all.

The next exercise helps you to connect to the universal energy of the sun, which represents the masculine energies of strength and courage, and gives you access to its powerful rays of light. When you focus on an energy source it will strengthen and enhance your own energy.

Exercise to connect to the power of the sun

✧ Close your eyes and relax.

✧ Put your hands on your stomach, covering your solar plexus. Think of the sun and imagine its powerful rays flowing down and connecting to your solar plexus.

✧ Lift off your hands and allow the energies to flow deeply within you. See yourself filled with the golden light that pours from the spiritual sun, bringing powerful energies to uplift your strength, courage and stamina. Feel yourself growing stronger and stronger as these bright golden rays fill you now. Let the power of it dissolve any anxiety or fears derived from your own concerns or those picked up from other people.

✧ Know that your sun – your solar plexus – and the universal sun are united and you can tap into this energy any time you want.

This chakra plays an important role in issues of personal power, for, as I mentioned, the solar plexus is involved with issues of fear, anxiety and inner strength. Through your will it enables your power of choice, courage, forcefulness, expansiveness and your ability to see beyond limitations, and governs all matters of spiritual growth. If we allow anxieties and fears to stay unresolved, eventually these negative energies act like poison and affect the physical organs around this centre. It has been noted that there is a correlation between problems with this chakra and the incidence of stomach conditions such as indigestion and ulcers.

Masculine energy

The energies that the solar plexus controls are masculine energies. Although they are normally dominant in men, they are part of the energetic make-up of all of us. We each hold both masculine and feminine energy. When you focus and develop your solar plexus chakra you are assisting in the empowerment of your masculine energy, which will help you to be stronger, more self-assured and courageous – all the characteristics that men traditionally have needed in order to fight their foes and bring in a supply of food. To reinforce these aspects for yourself as part of your empowerment plan I suggest you do this short exercise daily, to balance, develop and activate your solar plexus – rather as you would flex a muscle.

Exercise to develop and activate your solar plexus chakra

✧ Put your hand on your solar plexus and close your eyes.

✧ Picture the solar plexus chakra as a ball of yellow light. See the ball spinning into a perfect circle and getting brighter and brighter.

✧ See your sun shining powerful rays of light out to fill your entire aura. Know you are developing your strength and will as the yellow fire grows in size and power.

Here is a summary of the energy centres that govern the different aspects of your emotional and physical wellbeing.

	Purpose	Location	Colour
Crown	Works with issues of higher consciousness, our connection to the divine and universal energies	Top of the head	Purple
Third Eye	All aspects of seeing, both physical and inner sight. Intuition	Middle of the brow	Indigo
Throat	Your ability to express yourself and your sense of worth. All communication	Throat	Blue
Heart	Relates to all matters of love, giving and receiving. Compassion. Associated inner peace and happiness	Middle of the chest	Green, often with pink
Solar Plexus	Handles our ego, inner power, strength, will and identity	Below the ribs and above the navel	Yellow
Sacral	Relates to desires, sensations, sexuality, self-worth	Several inches below the navel	Orange
Base	Your sense of security and survival. Financial security and feeling at home	Base of spine	Red

Your chakras are sensitive to associated energies which can be accessed through your thoughts and imagination. Whenever you feel the need to strengthen your energy and wellbeing, you can use the following simple meditation.

Exercise to bring your entire energy field into balance and alignment

You are making a positive step into empowerment when you control the vibration and balance of your entire energy field. This exercise will give you that ability. Visualisation is a powerful tool that can be used effectively to strengthen and balance your energy centres. As you work with each chakra, place your hand on your body in the relevant position to help you hold your focus. I suggest you say the words in quotes out loud as the reverberation of your voice holds its own empowering force.

✧ Close your eyes and relax.

✧ Put your hand over your base chakra. Focus on this part of your body, your hips, your legs, your knees and your feet. Think of security and stability.

✧ See a red apple spinning. See it creating a perfect circle of red light. Say, 'I am grounded, I am secure and I put down my roots to stabilise myself in every way.'

✧ Place your hand on your sacral chakra, below your navel. Focus on the free flow of your digestive and urinary systems, the male and female reproductive organs and the fertility of creation. Remember you hold the energy of creation in spiritual and physical form. Your desires and wants spring from this location.

✧ See an orange spinning. See it creating a perfect circle of orange light. Say, 'I let my creative energies flow, I value myself, I acknowledge my skills and abilities.'

✧ Place your hand on your solar plexus, above your navel. Focus on your stomach and your free will, your ability to make your own choices, your strength and courage. From here you have the will to turn your desires into action.

✧ See a sun spinning. See it creating a perfect circle of yellow light. Say, 'I am strong, I am courageous, I claim my free will to determine my life. I release all confusion around my choices and I follow my dreams, goals and desires with love, fearlessly.'

✧ Place your hand on your heart centre in the middle of your chest. Focus on your heart and your lungs. This is the centre where love flows to others; remember to keep the doors of this centre wide open to enable you to receive love too.

✧ See a pink rose spinning. See it creating a perfect circle of pink light. Say, 'I love and accept myself and others, love flows freely in a perfect balance of give and take.'

✧ Place your hand on your throat. Focus on your throat and mouth and your ability to speak up and tell people what you feel. Focus on your ears and your patience and understanding to listen to others and be open to new ideas and inspiration.

✧ See a blue ball spinning. See it creating a perfect circle of blue light. Say, 'I speak my truth and express my feelings fearlessly.'

✧ Place your hand on your third eye in the centre of your forehead. Focus on your eyes, ears and nose. Your third eye gives you connection to your intuition, visionary abilities and psychic perceptions. Let your third eye hold the vision of your dreams and goals.

❖ See an indigo orb spinning into a perfect circle of the deepest violet blue light. Say, 'With love and positive intention I visualise my life moving forward to my greatest potential.'

❖ Place your hand on your crown chakra. Focus on your source of ideas and inspirations. This is your connection to universal energies and your own higher self that holds your own personal store of wisdom.

❖ See a purple sphere spinning, see it spin into a perfect circle of purple light. Say, 'I am in balance and harmony with myself and the universe, I am a being of spirit.'

THE EFFECT OF PLANTS AND NATURE ON YOUR ENERGY FIELD

Almost from day one of my awakening to the power of healing I have used essential oils to help in shifting and changing energy vibration, taking people out of negativity into a positive state. Essential oils are created from the extracts of plants, and their natural healing properties and the personality and energy vibration of each plant gives the oils specific intentions and powers of their own. For example, most of us are aware of the calming and relaxing effects of lavender and the uplifting effects and zing from the fragrance of lemon. Essential oils work hand in hand with your own intentions. For example, if you want to let go attachments, then you can use a blend that includes the powerful releasing and liberating extracts of Fennel, Myrtle and Spikenard. Throughout this book I suggest essential oils that you can use with a diffuser or oil burner to assist in some of the healing meditations and exercises. Full details of my own oil blends and the powers of plants to heal can be found on the Ripple website listed at the back of this book.

For the same reason, any connection with nature will have an effect on your mood. The vibrations of nature are constant – except where we have violated it with chemicals – and you can simply take a walk into a park or garden, stroll by the sea or touch a leaf and experience an instant shift in the vibration of your own energy. On your journey to full empowerment, take all the help you can – look for crystals, stones, plants, essences, food and fragrances that work for you. Simply choosing to use nature in your journey to well-being and strength is empowering.

We will now look at the various aspects that make up our personal power. Make your own list in your journal of the aspects of human nature that are your personal power. In the next section are a few that I have identified for you to develop in order to bring yourself into your fullest potential and set you free of limitations and inhibitions.

ASPECTS OF YOUR PERSONAL POWER

Your personal power can be seen in a variety of aspects – components that together create an amazing force. We will now look into these aspects, at their impact and what they can represent to you and your empowerment. We will see how you can develop your power of love, choice, self-responsibility, self-acceptance, manifestation, positive thinking and intuition.

THE POWER OF LOVE

Power is nothing but a driving force and its potential to improve your life and the lives of others is only unleashed when it is aligned with love. Many of the very powerful

characters who have taken the world stage are forces of darkness rather than of light. Hitler, Stalin and Mother Teresa all
worked with their personal power in full strength, but Mother
Teresa's power came from her heart. When you align your
power with love, you live through fearless love – what a
wonderful energy to infuse your thoughts, your emotions
and your intentions. When you live through the power of
love you radiate a force of light that positively affects your
relationship with yourself and others. It is the most effective
way to improve any issues you may have with self-esteem
and self-worth. It can also make decision making easier – as
I found when challenged by my own domestic troubles.

'The blend of strength and love is the most powerful force in
the world.'

Love is the antidote to fear

The world and our lives are full of threats and challenges
that can destabilise us as individuals and communities and
fill us with fear and confusion. These negative emotions can
make us act out of character, lead us to drugs, drink and
obsessive behaviour, and threaten our close relationships, work
and social life. Whenever you live through fear you are inclined
to make bad choices, behave badly, lose control and become
overwhelmed. My way to bring back a sense of calm and
control in my life when I am challenged is to change my
focus on the problem through the perspective of love. The
following visualisation is the one I used when I found myself
in anxiety and panic thanks to a series of overwhelming
family problems.

'Love is the most powerful force you can release.'

Exercise to align with the power of love and step into your heart

Use this exercise to escape from fear and to ensure your choices are made from the positive perspective of love. Your heart always speaks the truth to you, so take any problems and un-answered questions into your heart through this meditation.

✧ Close your eyes and relax your body, drop your shoulders and breathe deeply several times, deep into your stomach. As you breathe out, know you are letting go all tension, all stress, all frustration. As you breathe in, you become calmer, more rested and more relaxed.

✧ Focus on the centre of your chest; this is your emotional heart chamber where you deal with issues of love. See doors that open to allow you to step into a beautiful chamber.

✧ In the centre burns the flame of eternal love. Only posi-tive energies can exist here – energies of giving, sharing, comfort, nurture, kindness and compassion. You are surrounded and filled by aspects of love.

✧ Think of the problem that has been troubling you – let go all blame and judgement and see it and those involved through kindness and compassion.

✧ See beams of pink light representing love and compassion flow to the situation that is bothering you.

✧ Ask for help with ideas for resolution and ask for insights from your own higher spiritual aspects of wisdom and intu-ition. Know that there is a solution and be aware that when you are calm and collected this will come to you.

The many faces of love

The power of love can resolve issues, bring happiness and generally uplift your life. We expect love in relationships with our families and our partners, but there is also love waiting to be experienced in our relationships with friends and work colleagues. Love has many faces and aspects, and it will mean different things to different people depending on their personal experiences. If you have been brought up in care you may have missed the experience of a loving mother and father, but you may well have developed extraordinarily close relationships with friends, foster parents or care workers.

However, you may not see the love that has been and still is present in your life. I was brought up by a wonderful and actively loving mother and stepfather; my natural father left when I was young and never showed any concern or interest in me. I could easily have craved the love of my natural father and subsequently could have undervalued the loving care that my stepfather gave me. Luckily I did appreciate it and therefore was able to enjoy it to its fullest. However, it is easy to miss the love that is under your nose – you may take it for granted, fail to appreciate it, or even not see it as love of the kind you see others enjoying in the conventional relationships and happy families portrayed by television commercials.

Case study: The Power of You to find love everywhere

Jenny lost her mother when she was three years old. She was brought up by her father, who himself had mental and emotional problems. She was loved by him and her close family, but he was unable to truly open his heart and give her the emotional support she needed. As she grew into a teenager she could easily have fallen into the role of victim — 'I don't have parents who love me, I am different from other girls, nobody cares about me' and so on. This would have given her major issues to resolve — issues of self-worth, issues of abandonment and neglect, and issues to do with love and her lack of it. She may have sought love through sex and fulfilled her need through drugs, as so many of her peers have.

But fortunately she decided to seek love elsewhere. She made incredibly strong and profound relationships with people of her own age — she created a network of supportive and loving friends. Helped by the modern communication tools of Bebo, Facebook, texting and email, she was able to create and sustain a support network of love that was available to her all day and every day. By using her own power of initiative she recognised the love of her friends and learnt to value it. When her father recently had to go into hospital, she turned to her friends for support and they were there for her immediately.

Love is everywhere. It is in the support of friendship, the camaraderie of work colleagues, the interest and dedication of teachers, the smile of a stranger, the loyalty and companionship of pets, the beauty of nature. Do you see the love that is in your life? Look for it, access it, accept it, enjoy it and value it. The next exercise will give you the opportunity to think about where you can find love in your own life.

Exercise to find the power of love in your life

The essential oils of Rose and Geranium can help you attract love, heal the wounds of love and open you to receive love.

✧ First, write down the names of everyone who has ever shown you kindness, given you attention and listened to you, done something unexpected, or gone out of their way to make your life better in even the smallest way.

✧ Next, write down in your journal all those places you can go where you feel at peace or uplifted, and record all of those times when you felt filled with happiness, such as the birth of a baby, a special sunset, etc. These are moments filled with the love that comes from the universe – God's love.

Love nurtures you and is fuel for your personal power to grow. When we are loved we can blossom and grow from strength to strength, whereas when we are separated from love we shrivel up. Love may not always come packaged in the form we expect, but it is there.

YOUR POWER OF CHOICE

One of our greatest gifts, and one that places us apart from other sentient beings, is our ability to choose, to have free will. You are not programmed and your thoughts are your own. You can choose your beliefs and have your own feelings about the issues of the world. However, you may have been influenced in your life by the strong and dominant beliefs of other people; family members may have tried to enforce their will on you; the forceful arguments expressed through the media may have swayed your beliefs; religions and their influential leaders may have tried to control your thoughts; your own doubts may persuade you that you cannot achieve your dreams. Any of these situations can result in you giving away your most precious gift – the ability to make choices and decisions for yourself. And this can result in you losing some of your power. The good news is that you can reclaim what is yours. If you own your free will, if you believe that you have a choice, you immediately become stronger spiritually and emotionally.

'Free will is your greatest gift - please use it'.

FREE SPIRIT

To enjoy a true sense of freedom you need to exercise your right of choice and freedom in every part of your life. When you are dependent on others you are limiting your own life. When you rely on others to make decisions for you, you give away control and limit your free will. As I have said, spiritually, your free will, the right you have to choose, is one of your greatest gifts and only you can choose to act with it rather than be dominated by someone else's will.

Maybe you worry about making wrong decisions, making a bad choice or following the wrong path. From a spiritual perspective there are no wrong decisions, because whatever experience a particular choice brings will give you a chance to grow, to better understand other people and yourself, and will enrich your inherent wisdom. Every experience, whether seemingly positive or negative, will help you to become wiser. As parents we understand this. We know that if we never let our children try things for themselves, step out into the world or make up their own minds, they will never grow into independent and wise adults. This is a process that never stops – if you wish to continue to have a full and rich life you need to keep pushing the boundaries out further and further. You need to take yourself out of your comfort zone, try new experiences, take on challenges and expand your life as far as you possibly can. You cannot do that if you don't make decisions, if you sit on the fence, become apathetic about your life and the world in general or take the cautious route all the time. Be bold, step out of the box and set your spirit free.

Our minds and habits often limit how far we can push ourselves, mentally or physically. In yoga I am constantly amazed how much further my body will go when I let it. Here is an exercise to show you it is possible to go further than you believe you can.

Exercise to go beyond limiting boundaries

✧ Stand up and put your arm out straight in front of you.

✧ Hold your feet firm and twist around, look around and see how far you can go.

✧ Come back and drop your arm. Close your eyes, drop your shoulders and relax. Let the tension leave your body as you breathe in deeply four times.

✧ Now see yourself as a great tree with roots firmly connected into the Earth, and visualise yourself doing that exercise again. In your mind's eye see yourself going six inches further. Then one foot, then two. See how far your imagination will take you.

> ✧ Open your eyes and repeat the exercise. Notice the differ-
> ence. Well done!

*'As you step beyond limiting beliefs you are
exercising your power.'*

YOUR VOICE

As you have the right to choose you also have the right to
speak, to say what you feel. You claim your personal power
when you speak up for yourself, show your feelings and are
honest about your needs and desires: you become more
courageous, stronger, more determined, and you influence
both the way others perceive you and the way you perceive
yourself. This freedom of will and speech can be reflected
not only in your personal life but in your interactions with
the world around you.

There are many countries where personal freedoms are
seriously restricted. In Europe and America there were times
in the past when many of us would have been severely
limited in what we could do, discriminated against by our
social class, our religion, our sex, our race. Over the years
many individuals and groups have stood up and demanded,
even fought for, our rights, pushing open doors that were
barred, giving their lives for our freedom, campaigning for
justice and equality. For sure there are still restrictions and
injustice, but do you actually make the most of the freedoms you do have?

EXPRESSING YOUR POWER OF CHOICE

You empower yourself when you express your needs, beliefs
and choices and there are many ways in which you can

express and utilise your powers of choice and speak out. Here are some you might consider.

Make the most of your rights
You have the right to vote. Use this vote, ladies – in the past women died so that we could have this right. Each vote does count.

You have the right to education. In some countries parents will give their entire wealth to enable their children to have what to them is a most valuable asset – a good education. Make the most of any free education on offer. Enrich yourself through knowledge. Understanding, knowledge and wisdom are powerful tools in life; they open the doors to maximising your greatest potential and living a more fulfilling life.

You have the right to march, petition and lobby. If you want things to change in the world around you, then use these rights. When our government is making decisions that you feel passionate about and if they are not offering a people's vote – a referendum – then get out and march. If more of us had shown our disapproval of the Iraq war maybe we could have stopped it happening. Set up forums on the internet to find people with the same intentions and write to newspapers; use Facebook and Twitter to network.

Be bold with your choices
At home and in relationships, remember to speak up about your feelings when you can, rather than suppressing them. If you hold your thoughts to yourself, no one can really know the true you and what you want. How can others meet your needs when they don't know what you truly feel?

When you are making a choice, listen to your instinct, your gut feeling, your intuition, and courageously make a decision. Procrastination is negative and debilitating – it will slow you down and weaken your resolve. Use the method of entering your heart centre I gave you in the previous section (p. 27) to ensure your choices are fearless and based on your truth.

To connect with your inner feelings, focus on your solar plexus, open your heart and make a choice from within, rather than just from your thoughts and logic. Remember that it is better to make a decision, even if you have to change direction at a later stage, than be stuck at a cross-roads making no progress at all.

You step fully into your power when you utilise your free will and make your own decisions without being influenced by other people. As you make your own way in life and choose to be independent and self-reliant you gain strength and self-respect.

THE POWER OF SELF-RESPONSIBILITY

One of the most empowering things you can do is to take full responsibility for yourself. This means being independent, making your own choices and acknowledging that only you can be responsible for your own happiness. If you rely on others to make you happy, then you are admitting that they can control how you feel about life. If you have ever in your life given away this control, you will know how vulnerable you can be when you rely on someone else either to make decisions for you or to be the meter of your happiness count. To take the initiative now, you need to show your commitment to become your own master and set this out in an intention.

'Being self-responsible is being in control.'

Say out loud your intention to be in control of your own destiny. Use a mantra or affirmation along these lines: 'I am in control of my life, my feelings, my choices and my destiny.' Repeat it over and over again and, when you can, shout it out loud! Remember the universe responds to your needs and intentions, whether they are positive or negative, so keep a positive vibe in your responses to everything that you come across and in every request you put out.

There is one state or sense that can sabotage your efforts to take responsibility for your own happiness and your life outcomes, and that is the sense of being a victim. If you feel that life has treated you badly, that you are the victim either of other people's actions or of their attitudes, then you may find that this control slips through your fingers. You may have had an experience that has made you a genuine victim – of crime, of abuse, of discrimination, etc. However, once you have moved beyond the emotional fallout of the experience you need to let go blame. If you get stuck in the state of being a victim and holding on to blame, you will not be able to fulfil your life and the outcome of your life experience will leave you weakened rather than strengthened.

What you can do to take responsibility for yourself

First, you can be courageous and bold and step away from blame. Let go blaming your parents and seeing how they treated you as a child as the cause of your current problems. Decide to set yourself free by taking control of your life and your feelings from this moment on. Rather than blaming the government for the country's problems, get involved in the decision-making process or put forward your views.

Try to do your bit to dissolve the need for the nanny culture. If you take personal responsibility for avoiding broken paving stones, or for the fact that hot water comes from hot taps, then this mindset will lose momentum and common sense can return!

If you are not happy at work, don't blame your boss or your colleagues. Make a conscious decision either to make the most of your work or to look for another position. When you take up a new job, visualise yourself surrounded by supportive people. Be open-hearted and friendly from day one and take a positive vibe to work. Remember, light energy attracts light energy.

Listen to yourself and your friends and notice when any one of you starts playing the blaming game. Nip it in the bud. It is a negative habit and when you play it you pass the responsibility for your life, health, happiness and success right into the hands of someone else – the self-responsible route is the one to your personal power.

Just be careful. Avoid taking on the responsibility of other people and becoming a controller. Everyone has free will and you should not make decisions for anyone else except children or those who are completely incapacitated. Otherwise you will become burdened and you will be breaking the spiritual law of free will, which is:

Everyone is responsible for their own actions and outcomes.

Claiming and owning

When you are stepping into the power of self-responsibility, you can claim and own aspects of your life that you may have left dormant or passed into the responsibility of other people. It's easy to hand over too much responsibility at work, for example, when you have delegated a task to someone else. I have a fairly busy life, like most people, and where I can I have learnt to delegate as much as possible. But in that delegation I have found at times that I have passed too much over, so that I don't feel associated with the situation any more.

Is there any part of your life that you have let go into the hands of another person but which is ultimately your own responsibility? Recognise what is ultimately your responsibility and own it. Make a list of aspects of your life that you know are your responsibility. Decide how you are going to claim them again and make a note to keep a monitoring eye open for everything on the list, even roles, tasks or situations you have delegated.

THE POWER OF SELF-ACCEPTANCE AND KNOWING YOURSELF

You can become strong and powerful by understanding, knowing and accepting yourself without judgement. This means accepting your personality, character and crucially your spiritual aspect. To allow this acceptance you need to realise that you are not just your mind, your emotions and your body. In my book *The Soul Connection* I showed the link between ourselves and spirit. Our spiritual essence is unconditional love. Our spiritual essence has the ability to create. We are spiritually created from the energy of Source – the energy of God. This is the true essence of all human beings and it is a wonderful, amazing and beautiful energy that is dazzling and light. Like our power, it is easy to lose sight of our true core energy as it is masked by the unfinished business, the negative emotions we still carry from past experiences. We develop coping mechanisms, behaviour and attitudes that help us manage inner pain and disturbed feelings and these 'coping coats' become so much a part of us that it is easy to mistake them for our true self. I will be looking at the effects of these 'coping coats' on ourselves and other people, how they affect our lives and how we can release them, in the next chapter. For now I want to focus on your underlying energy, that no matter how deeply it is hidden, or covered in coping coats and managing strategies, it always remains love.

RELEASING JUDGEMENT

You can be truly in your power when you are happy with who you are, comfortable with yourself, at ease with all aspects of yourself, accepting of your strengths and weaknesses and content with the role you play in life. It is very easy to fall into a critical attitude about yourself. In order to help you avoid doing so, hold in mind these pointers to self-acceptance and self-love:

✧ Your failures in life do not make you a failure – failures are opportunities to learn.

✧ Judgement made by yourself and others is not a true measure of your value – it is simply a judgement.

✧ If you see yourself through a mask of judgement and criticism, you are not seeing clearly.

✧ Don't judge yourself against others – you are unique and you have the skills and attributes that you need for this lifetime and the role you are to play here.

✧ Don't be influenced by an image-conscious society – your true worth is in what you do, not what you look like.

Take some time out to be contemplative about yourself. The next exercise will help you to focus on your positive aspects – your skills, your attitudes and your strengths.

Exercise to connect to your strengths

❖ Get into your heart centre before you start to write (use the exercise on p. 27), so that you are not perceiving yourself from anything else but love.

❖ Allow time to consider your strengths, your skills, your best attributes, and make a note of them in your journal. See how these are used in your work and pastimes.

❖ Give yourself credit for any strengths or attributes that you have acquired and those that you have gained from the experiences of your life, whether or not these experiences seemed negative or even disastrous at the time.

❖ Against each strength and skill write down how you can develop this further and how you can use it more extensively in your life either at work, at home or through an activity. Think about how you can use them to benefit yourself and other people.

❖ Any time when you feel down, feel inadequate, feel worthless, please take out this list and read it. Bless you!

THE POWER OF STRENGTH AND COURAGE

As we can see in the story of Joe Simpson, there are times when we can touch within ourselves an extraordinary resource of courage and physical strength. You may never be physically tested to such a degree unless you practise extreme sports and activities. However, you will almost certainly need courage at some time in your life. You may need courage to speak up – either for yourself, for a belief, or for the sake of someone else. You may need courage to be honest when you know there will be unpleasant repercussions. You may need courage to face a fear, like speaking in public. You may need courage to make a change that will take you out of your comfort zone – like changing your job or leaving a partner.

Case study: The Power of You with courage

Debbie is an inspiration for courage and the strength to let go and follow a dream. After twelve years of a relationship that was at best giving her 50 per cent, she decided to cut loose and step forward in life alone. It took great courage to make the step and many tears were shed, but she did it and set herself free. She gave up her home and sold everything – and I mean everything. She had a dream to help animals and children, so she took herself off to Sri Lanka to help at an orphanage for a month and then spend time at an elephant sanctuary.

During her stay she became incensed at the state of the country's dogs, who were, like many animals in Asia, lacking support and often ill-treated. She had always been a dog lover and she couldn't sleep at night thinking of the pitiful state of the dogs she had seen. Having become obsessed with her dream to help them, she came back to the UK and spent some months raising funds to enable her to go back and work with a small dog rescue centre. She had no idea how she would support herself until three weeks before she left, when an email arrived offering her a paid position with the charity.

Her aim is not only to help with the physical wellbeing of the dogs but to help educate the children about animal care by taking dogs to visit schools. She has become happy and fulfilled – her courage to step away from all she knew and take a step into the unknown has turned her life around. She is now exhilarated with life; doing wonderful work and living to her greatest potential. Bless her.

There are many times when you will need your courage. Maybe you'll never face such a huge life change as Debbie's, but every day you will face challenges that need strength and determination.

Exercise to strengthen resolve and courage

Essential oils that can help are Ginger and Cedar.

✧ Close your eyes and relax.

✧ Place your hand on your solar plexus – your energy centre for strength and courage, the seat of your personal power. Think of the situation you face and visualise yourself in it, or sense that you have it before you.

✧ Send beams of golden light from your solar energy to the situation. Know you are infusing it with your inner strength.

✧ See the sun sending down beams of golden energy to fill you and replenish your resources of courage. Know that this energy is infinite and everlasting and you can tap into it as long as you like.

✧ Feel yourself filled with the golden light of strength and know that every fibre and cell of your body is strengthened and empowered – you can take on the world!

'Everyone has courage and strength - it may be hidden but it is there inside you.'

THE POWER OF MANIFESTING – CREATING YOUR DREAMS

You have the ability and power to attract into your life what-ever you desire. As I said earlier, your spirit is created from universal creative energy, which means that every one of us has the ability to create and manifest our dreams, desires and needs. This power comes from the intention of your will, which is your personal power to choose, and the energy of your thoughts. If your thoughts are affected in any way by anxiety or fear, then the energy you send out as your inten-tion is also going to be affected – in other words, you will be sending out negative intentions which then draw towards you negative situations, people and experiences.

As you unlock your power base – your solar plexus energy – you open the way to the greater power of the universal energies of will and creation. Effectively you connect to the spiritual power of manifesting. This means you will find that your powers to bring into reality what you want and need become faster and more effective – so much so that you will be amazed how one minute you say this is what you want, and in no time at all there it is before you!

When I started my charity Hearts and Hands for Africa, I needed £20,000 for its registration in the UK. This would have taken all my savings, so I decided to attract the money. I happened to be on holiday in Italy at around that time, so I went inside every church I passed, lit a candle and used my manifesting process (see the next exercise). On the way home from the airport I had a strong sense of a major gift coming my way. I told my friend Brenda, who was travelling with me, 'I think there will be a cheque waiting for me at home.' When I arrived, there on the kitchen table sat a pile of mail, and in the middle was a letter from the national Premium Bond office telling me I had won £5,000! The next day I was given a £5,000 cheque as repayment of a long-term loan I had made to a friend, and the following day my husband handed me a cheque for £10,000, the profit from a business venture that he had promised for me for the charity. Absolutely amazing – but it left me wondering if I should have upped the amount to £50,000!

It's OK to want money if you need it for something special, but I have found that the more universally benefi-cial the request, the easier it will be to materialise it. My friend Sue Stone (see her book *Love Life, Live Life* in the appendix) manifested a home, a horse and a business. Nina Ferguson, the publisher of my books in Norway, recently manifested a garage within two days, and garages are like gold dust in Oslo. The following exercise will show you the way I put out my intentions without them being affected by any negative expectations or influences – be careful to include the last step and remember to keep holding your intention clear and consistent, as any wavering will muddle the outward flow of your thoughts and your intentions will lose their clarity. Be careful what you ask for and make sure that it is for your highest good. If you manifest desires that are materially driven or attached to greed or ego, then they may not bring the happiness you expect.

Exercise to manifest and create your dreams from thought and intention

✧ Write down your intention, your goal or what it is you

want to manifest, create or materialise. Consider carefully the ramifications of this in your life. Say it out loud three times and see if it rings true to you. Does it sound good? Don't share it with other people at this time as their attitudes towards your dream may affect you.

✧ Hold your written request close to your heart centre and visualise or, if you find visualising difficult, know that you are entering through the doors of your heart. These doors are the symbolic opening of your heart chakra. As you see them open, step inside.

✧ From your heart, see your request materialising. If it's money you want, then visualise a symbol of money such as golden coins pouring into your lap, or see a cheque being handed to you. If you are taking an exam see yourself receiving a diploma as a sign of success. See your dream in action and reality.

✧ Draw the symbol below — it was given to me by my spirit guides, who come to me in meditation. It sends out the vibration of intention to materialise thoughts.

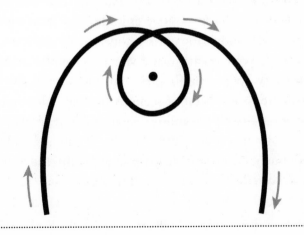

> ✧ Now hand this process over to the universal energies of
> creation. Let go the way in which your dream and vision
> will be created – in other words, don't sit there day after
> day wondering or worrying how it's going to happen! Simply
> let it go into divine timing and divine powers. I symbolically
> cut cords of attachment by chopping one hand on the
> other as I release my attachment to the outcome.

When you have success please let me know – I will add
your story to the Power of You website, which is full of the
inspirational experiences people have had using their powers
to manifest.

*'Energy attracts like energy, positive intentions attract
positive experiences.'*

THE POWER OF POSITIVE THINKING

Manifesting requires control of your thoughts, in order to
make sure they are positive and supportive. Positive thinking
is a habit that you can develop, and one that can change
your life. Not only do positive attitudes and thoughts allow
you to create and bring into reality what you want, they
will also lift your spirits, make you feel happier and affect
you in every way – mind, spirit and body.

If you are in the habit of seeing your cup half empty and
find it easier to be pessimistic, then you might like to ask
yourself why this is so. Could you be frightened of hoping
for too much in case you are disappointed with the outcome?
Are you scared that your hopes for success will be dashed?
Do you think you are not really good enough to have the
very best in life? Our thoughts are one of our most powerful

assets, because with practice we can control them. Whatever is the subject of your focus receives the energy that flows from you. This means that positive thoughts of love, kindness, caring, interest, excitement and other energies that hold a high vibration and are uplifting flow through your energy field and affect both yourself and the recipient of your attention. If you think of a family member with affection, both of you benefit. You will both feel lighter, refreshed and even happier.

Before I start a workshop I deliberately uplift the energies of the room so that people arriving step into a positive atmosphere. I do this by setting my intention – which, I may remind you, is a positive thought with a purpose – to fill the room with love and uplifting energies. I am sensitive to energies because I am a healer, so I feel the change in seconds. I also call in universal energies to help the positive vibrations of the room, and this happens almost immediately too. I visualise the entire world as a being in its own right and I see myself as a cell in that greater being – this way I can understand how we all are part of the same energy. When you align and open yourself to the universal energies of love, joy and positive experience, you have access to the infinite and powerful forces that collude with your intentions.

I will be exploring this concept in later chapters when we see how we can be affected by mass consciousness: the combined thoughts and energies of everyone in the world. If you generally struggle to stay positive, I will also be addressing some of the reasons and causes of personal negativity. Right now, though, let's see how you can begin to develop a new habit of thinking in a positive manner.

Exercise to develop the power of positive thinking

Bergamot essential oil can help with positivity.

✧ Sit in your room or garden. Ask the universal energies of positivity and enlightenment to assist you in this exercise.

✧ Take a look at a single object and give it your full attention. See all the positive aspects of that object, what it does for you, its colour, shape and style. Ignore anything about it that would normally annoy you – imagine a beam of positive light leaving you and filling the object.

✧ Do this for any number of things in your home.

✧ Now think of the people in your family. Again, think of all their positive attributes. If a negative thought comes in, just put it to one side, say, 'Yes, but . . .' and think another positive thought. Send love and beams of light directly to each person.

✧ Now think of yourself and all your own positive attributes. Call in beams of light from the universal energies to fill you.

✧ Next, think of your situation in life. Again, focus only on the positives – we will deal with the negatives later. See each situation filled with your light and the light of the universe.

✧ Accept that you are filled with positive energy, that this will now fill every aspect of your life as you open your eyes and return to the room.

Practise this whenever you have a few moments to spare – before you sleep, travelling in a train or as a car passenger, waiting in the dentist's and so on. Eventually it will become a habit to see the positive instead of immediately stepping into pessimistic, critical and negative thinking.

CREATING AN UPLIFTING AND POSITIVE MINDSET

Here are more ways that you can uplift your mind, body and spirit:

✧ Read uplifting books, like the stories in *Chicken Soup for the Soul*.

✧ Watch inspirational videos and clips. There are many on the web, but here are two sites that you may enjoy: www.webstudio13.com, which includes the thirteen most inspiring YouTube videos of all time, as well as many short clips, and www.achievezine.com.

✧ Use positive affirmations. Say something strong and positive, out loud, to remind yourself of your achievements, your strengths, the blessings of your life, the state that you wish to achieve. Always make the statement in the present and start with I AM, for this is the inner condition of you, and expresses the intention of claiming it for yourself. For example: 'I am growing healthier day by day. I am in my power and all is possible. I am grateful for the love of my family and friends.'

✧ Focus on love and acceptance – love of yourself, love of others and love of life. Make every day an opportunity to give love to someone. Love can be translated into caring, kindness, acceptance without judgement, tolerance, encouragement, giving, sharing, inspiring someone, giving hope.

THE ONE THAT GETS AWAY

There will be times when, despite all your efforts, you will have negative thoughts. You will worry about a family member, see the downside of a situation or feel irritable towards a loved one. If you want to negate the thoughts you have just had, then here is a quick and easy method of transforming the energy of your thought from negative/dark to positive/light:

> *Once you have consciously recognised that a negative thought has escaped, send a beam of positive energy in the form of light to catch it, encompass it and transform it. Light is more powerful and stronger than darkness, so your beam of light will always disperse a negative thought form. You are now back in control of your thoughts!*

We have now learnt that we can utilise the power of our will to change the way we think and feel, and that we can control our mindset. Now let's see how we can access one of our most powerful assets – our intuition.

THE POWER OF INTUITION

Intuition is our power source of wisdom, one that we accumulate and store from all we have experienced in this and previous lifetimes. It is a spiritual database that is beyond our conscious memory but is still accessible and can be used to assist us to make decisions. Women are usually more prepared to acknowledge this power than men, although the masculine take on this is 'gut feeling'. It is also referred to as a sixth sense – even by those who don't acknowledge their powerful spiritual aspect at all.

I will be discussing ways to utilise your intuition in later chapters, when we see how we can use our powers in daily life, but here I want to share a way that you can focus on the source of this wisdom and how you can align yourself to it. This following exercise, and the whole subject of your spiritual energy that is this higher source of knowledge and understanding – sometimes described as your Higher Self, Higher Consciousness, I AM Self or Oversoul – is more fully explained in my book *The Soul Connection*. This illustration shows the energetic connection you have to this unseen source of wisdom.

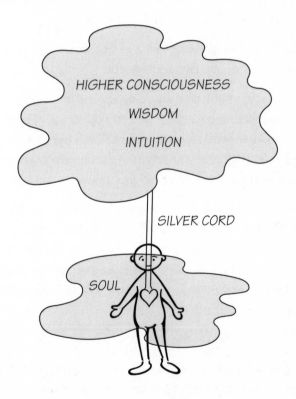

**Connection to the intuition of your
Higher Consciousness**

Meditation to access your power of intuition — aligning to your Higher Self

In this meditation we use symbols to represent the access and source of your Higher Self or Higher Consciousness. Essential oils that can help are Frankincense, Sandalwood or Jasmine.

✧ Close your eyes and relax, drop your shoulders.

✧ See yourself as a great tree with your roots growing deep into the Earth beneath you. This connection to the Earth makes you strong, grounded and stable.

✧ See the doors of your heart and step inside. This takes you away from doubt, fear and anxiety.

✧ See a silver flight of stairs rising up and allow yourself to follow these steps as they take you up to your Higher Self and your personal store of wisdom. Climb higher and higher, higher and higher as you pass from the dense physical dimensions into the spiritual and higher realms of your being.

✧ See a white building, light and shining. This is your personal library, the holder of the knowledge and understanding you have accumulated through the entire journey of your soul. Step into your library and see the wealth of knowledge and understanding you have amassed through your experiences.

✧ Ask any question — the answer lies here.

✧ Know that your heart, your soul and your Higher Self are aligned and connected. Any time you need guidance, your Higher Self can provide a response.

> ✧ Take time to listen to your answers. Don't be concerned
> if they do not come instantly, you may find them arriving
> in the next few days as ideas and thoughts drop in to help
> you.

THE POWER OF RESILIENCE

Our human spirit – the force that flows through every one
of us and is the energy of our personal power – has the
ability to resist all manner of challenges and put-downs. In
the rest of this book we will be looking at some of these
challenges and exploring how you can manage and withstand their negative force. Each challenge will require you
to dig deep and find your courage and strength. No matter
how strong you become, however, there will be times when
you will be pushed down and will feel yourself becoming
weak and disempowered. Earlier in this book I described the
way I coped with my feeling of weakness and sense of being
overwhelmed by going into my heart centre, but there are
a number of ways in which you can connect to the power
of resilience that is within you and which will give you both
the ability to bounce back, to get up when you have fallen,
and the determination to continue towards your goal.

First, keep your eyes and focus on your goal and see any
setback as a learning experience, something that may well one
day prove useful. In the next chapter we will look more closely
at the process of growth through experience. Consider the
way animals manage setbacks. They get up and go forward
unless seriously disabled. It is part of our human condition to
sit around and allow ourselves to be disempowered by issues
of blame, self-worth, etc.

Next, connect to and focus on your solar plexus and do the exercises at the beginning of this chapter to reinforce your will and courage. Visualise yourself as a river that is constantly making its way to the sea. Notice the way that you go over and around the rocks that are the obstacles in your path. Know that your human spirit is like the stream – it will get there one way or another. If one path is closed, there is always another to try. Keep working on the exercises in this chapter to ensure that you hold and maintain all aspects of your personal power from day to day.

In the next chapter we will look at some of the reasons you may struggle with self-worth, self-esteem and confidence, and at the greatest saboteurs of your power – stress, anxiety, fear and paranoia.

TWO

Do You Sabotage Your Power?

In this chapter I will help you to understand how you may have become disempowered. We will look at why you may find it difficult to access the powers that we have just explored. We will see why you may have buried your true self beneath layers of coping coats, developed to manage the shock, trauma, rage or guilt that can be the result of negative experiences. We will see how fear, from stress through to paranoia, limits your power, disenabling you and weakening your resolve and inner strength. And we will see how your own thoughts, attitudes and emotions can negatively affect you and your power force.

The emotion that blocks our progress, that limits us the most, is fear, so let's tackle this first. The mildest form of fear is stress. I am sure that you have felt the butterflies-in-the-stomach sensation that comes from anxiety or experienced the stabbing and debilitating dread that sears through the solar plexus, up and down your body, when you are in a state of fear.

STRESS

Stress is a symptom that you are not coping with a life that is too full, overwhelming or painful. We often get stressed when we don't allow enough time to complete our plans, when we are overextended at work or when our finances are running away with us. Stress is caused by a constant, chronic situation of difficulty and can build up over time.

THE SYMPTOMS OF STRESS AND ANXIETY

Do you suffer any of these symptoms?

✧ sweaty hands

✧ panic attacks

✧ butterflies in the stomach

✧ adrenaline rushes that start by making you feel strong then leave you weak

✧ the 'Oh my God, I'll never manage this' feeling and sense of inadequacy

Triggers for stress include:

✧ doing work you don't enjoy or which is outside your skill set;

✧ a major life change, for example getting married or divorced, retirement, redundancy, parenthood, moving house or, worse still, changing country, career change;

✧ too much responsibility without enough support;

✧ being overwhelmed by family matters;

✧ juggling home, parents, children and work concerns;

✧ financial worries;

✧ health problems;

✧ antisocial behaviour in your local environment.

WHAT YOU CAN DO

Some of these situations can be ameliorated by making a necessary change in your life or lifestyle, while for more serious causes you may need help from experts, counsellors or therapists. All, however, are signs of being overwhelmed. Wherever and whenever possible, keep your life simple. I used to juggle so many roles that I was constantly in danger of dropping some of the balls, if not all of them. Since then I've learnt that I can manage my time more effectively if I box or partition work, family time and 'me time'. If you keep strong boundaries and manage your time and space, you will avoid situations where you hurtle around, bouncing off the walls, your heart beating overtime, and managing to do nothing well. I call this 'getting into my box of the moment'.

There are many other ways that you can handle and prevent stress. Breathe deeply, down into your stomach – this is where anxieties and nervousness sit. With each breath, visualise yourself letting go the stresses and strains of the day. As you breathe in, imagine you are taking in calming energies that will act as a balm to your disharmony.

Symbolically release the burdens of responsibility that sit heavily on your shoulders by sweeping them away with your

hands. Visualise rocks dropping away as each burden or responsibility you carry falls away. You can also help your work
colleagues by doing this for them, it's most soothing.

Allow plenty of time for your plans. Work out the worst-
case scenario whenever you schedule a journey or project.
Make allowances for other people, late deliveries and slow
work. When planning a journey, allow for the worst traffic
conditions and take a book – if you have a wait at the other
end, at least you can relax and enjoy some quiet time.

Take breaks during the day, as well as holidays. It's essential to give yourself 'nothing time', or time to do things
outside your normal routine. The change will refresh you
and allow you to come back strengthened to your everyday
life.

Massage and yoga are good for stress, as both help you to
unwind your body and mind. Exercise and physical activity,
meanwhile, will stop your mind going into burnout. Vigorous
exercise and sport will take your attention away from your
worries.

Delegate and share your workload and responsibilities
when you can. Being Superman or Superwoman just attracts
stress. I go into meltdown when I take on too many projects and then I can't do any of them satisfactorily. Know
your limits and learn to say 'no' to any extra workload. Create
strong boundaries; know when to say 'no' or 'later'. It's not
rude to say 'no' as long as you do it with a pleasing manner,
but it can make the difference to your health and state of
mind.

'Being calm and centred is a state of empowerment.'

BEING IN THE MOMENT

A great antidote to stress is to bring yourself truly into the present and focus on something other than your problems. Any hobby or interest that takes you out of yourself will do this. I recently found a great, creative way to step back and refocus which costs nothing and can be aesthetically pleasing as well. The activity is a form of Zen meditation called Stone Balancing.

The concept is based on putting stones on top of each other at their point of balance. As everything has a point of balance, it is possible to mount the most unlikely pieces on top of each other. Start with small stones and go from there. I find it extremely relaxing and when you get the balance it feels amazing. It is impossible to do this without becoming totally absorbed and forgetting all your troubles! To read more about Stone Balancing, visit the website of Andrew Gray, a master in the art, listed in the appendix.

Finally, here is an exercise to help you unwind and relax.

Meditation to relax

Use this meditation to calm you down at any time. If you have trouble with sleeping, it can be employed when you go to bed.

✧ Drop your shoulders, let go your frown.

✧ Visualise yourself surrounded by a protective flame of purple.

✧ See yourself as a tree with roots growing deep into the Earth beneath you, holding you strong and grounded.

✧ Visualise yourself beside a lake surrounded by mountains.

You dangle your bare feet into the water – it feels cool and refreshing. Overhead, white birds fly through a blue sky. The lake is totally calm and reflects the mountains and sky. Sense the peace and calm atmosphere from the stillness of the water.

✧ Breathe deeply four times right through the bottom of your lungs to your stomach.

✧ The peaceful and relaxing energies of the lake gently move up from your feet, up your legs, through your thighs and into your hips. Every muscle relaxes and all tension leaves you.

✧ The energy relaxes every vertebra and muscle in your back as it moves up to your shoulders. Your shoulders bear the force of responsibility – lift and drop your shoulders several times, then linger awhile as the tension seeps away with the tranquil energy from the lake.

✧ Serenity moves up through your neck and fills your head, brain and face. Every muscle in your face relaxes.

✧ The energy moves down your front, through your arms, into your hands and right to the end of your fingers. Flex and stretch your fingers as you release the anxieties and frustrations that are stored there.

✧ Sense all fears, worries and troubling issues. Breathe deeply again and as you breathe out see them gently flow away from you into the lake, where they are dispersed in its serene and tranquil waters.

✧ Continue with the deep breathing for a few moments while you let go all tension.

FEAR

Stress is a common, everyday problem, but many of us also have to manage fear.

Fear is the most debilitating of all the emotions – some people say it's the furthest point from love. It certainly takes all our power. There are many things that cause us to become fearful and at any time we are probably managing any number of situations that challenge us. We all need courage to face our fears, whatever they may be.

Fear can block your path completely. It can weaken you and it can make you act out of character. It can also be sneaky – it will put thoughts into your head that make you think of all sorts of reasons why you cannot do things. You will find yourself saying you are too busy, too stressed, too poor, too sick to do something, even though it may be something you say you want to do. The truth is that you fear to do it.

For example, many people are frightened to be what they really want to be because they are deeply scared that people will laugh at them, that they are not good enough, that they will be judged, won't succeed, won't reach the levels of perfection they seek, will be scorned or put down. They will then make up any number of excuses. And in fact their body will collude – just when you are about to run the marathon that you have been training for weeks to take part in, you will twist an ankle or break a toe. Fear of stepping into your dream often affects your knees, hips and feet – all physical symptoms of moving forward. Take your journal and take time to identify your own fears. What stops you moving forward? What makes you feel weak and helpless? Are there situations that you avoid through fear?

'Experience it, process it, absorb it, understand it, grow and then move on.'

WHAT YOU CAN DO ABOUT FEAR

Ask yourself the following questions:

✧ Is this a real threat or an old insecurity being triggered by a current situation? Sometimes our memories of past experiences can create fears which we superimpose on our current situation. Check that your fear is based on a real situation you face rather than a memory.

✧ Is the fear worse than the threat? As the saying goes, we often fear the fear more than the situation itself. Are you getting anxious because it seems that you are under threat? Check out the facts.

✧ Are you being hooked up into the drama and hype? Are you being affected by those around you or by the media?

✧ What can you gain or learn from this? Every challenge in life brings its lessons – what are you going to learn from your particular fear?

Once you have identified the fears that control your life, then you can work on letting them go. There are a number of steps you can take to clear and release your fears:

Step up and face it. When you come face to face with something you fear and step towards it bravely, it quite often becomes less of a monster than you had imagined. You can spend many sleepless nights worrying about a situation, only to find that on the day it's not nearly as bad as you feared. If you run away from the object of your fear it will take control of you. If you face it, you are in control.

Build up your strength through positivity, resolve, determination. A positive attitude is a huge advantage when getting through difficult situations. Use an affirmation along these lines: 'I am in control', 'I am bigger than this situation', 'I am courageous', 'I can overcome', etc. If you receive a setback, if you meet challenges, if you are scared – think of one of your role models, keep your focus on your goal and keep going. Dust yourself off and have another attempt.

Think of the story of the tortoise and the hare – the tortoise kept focus and won the race, while the hare became distracted and lost. Keep reminding yourself of your goal, see yourself on the other side of the adversity or the fear. Keep focused. Have your goal and your affirmations posted on your fridge or your office wall. Overcoming fear is a way to make yourself stronger and wiser.

See your fear through the perspective of love. Love is the most powerful force in the universe, and light and love can overcome darkness. As you turn on a light in a dark room, the darkness will always be dispelled. Use the exercises I have already given you to step into your heart. Fear comes from a dark place, it is a heavy energy – if you face it with love and the strength of your will, you will be coming from a light, energised and strong place.

The next exercise will give you more help to make this shift, to let your fears go.

Exercise to let go your attachment to a memory that creates fear

Essential oils or incense that can help are Fennel, Myrtle or Spikenard.

✧ Write down a list of the fears you are ready to let go. Tie a thread around your wrist to represent each of these fears.

✧ Close your eyes and relax. Visualise yourself going back through the adult years of your life. When you come to the cause of your fear, break the thread and with the power of your intention let the fear go out of your life and your mind. Say out loud, 'I release my attachment to my fear of . . .'

✧ Do this through your life, going back through your teens, your childhood, your baby years, right to the time of your conception.

FEAR OF THE FUTURE

While we are looking at the effects of fear, I should mention a fear that comes up in the world from time to time – the fear that the world is coming to an end. The latest scare story that has taken hold is that the world will end in 2012. Much of this speculation began with the discovery that the calendar kept by the ancient priests of the Mayan civilisation in South America ended in the year 2012. It is predicted among other things that many of Earth's inhabitants will be taken away to another planet. The stories vary, from spaceships taking away the 'good' to major floods, through natural disasters and devastation killing most of the inhabitants of Earth, to an Ascension whereby the 'saved' will leave – this last relating to the apocalyptic Bible story from the Book of Revelation.

I personally believe that there will be change around that time. But I believe that the predominant energy of the world will change from dark to light, which will mean it will be easier to love than to hate, to create peace than war, and that the heavy energies of anger, guilt, mistrust and fanatical hate will subside, allowing us to live more harmoniously with each other. Currently the entire planetary energy field is filled with overpowering negative thought forms created from our fears. Thought forms are the condensed energies of similar vibrations, collecting together to create a dense mass similar to a thundercloud – they affect us all and make it difficult for us to keep our spirits and energy uplifted and positive. However, I am optimistic about the future of humanity and the world and feel that there are enough individuals who are positively bringing light and love to lift us above the fear and hate that dominates just now.

'Don't be pulled into hype - keep calm.'

THE CHALLENGE OF SCARY STORIES

Hype and scary stories sell newspapers. The Western media is full of negativity – looking on the downside, wallowing in gloom, cups half empty, focusing more on crime than on good deeds and the wonderful things people do for each other every day. When the energies of our world have tipped from being predominantly negative to predominantly positive we will know, because then the papers will be filled with optimistic and upbeat news. In the meantime, use your discretion about what you read and what you allow yourself to believe. Keep your own thoughts positive by focusing on your friends, family and work: look for the good news and focus on that. When I find the news too depressing I turn off the TV and find a radio channel that's playing music to lift me up.

The primal approach to a threat is either to stand and fight or run like hell. While it might feel good to run and hide under the duvet, there are many times when fear pervades our homes and gets into our minds. At that point we just have to deal with it, or it will take us over and become paranoia. When you are scared by something you have heard or read in the media and your mind won't accept logic, you need courage and strength to prevent yourself being overwhelmed by fear. This kind of fear is fear of the future and of what *may* happen, so you need to firmly root yourself in the present. If you are to remain able to see through the hype to the truth, you need to be grounded, stable and connected to reality, so that your mind does not run riot with everything you read. Here is a meditation that can help you ground yourself and connect to your personal power of courage and strength.

Exercise for courage and stability to handle fear of the future

✧ Close your eyes and relax.

✧ Visualise yourself sitting on a bench in the courtyard in the centre of a castle. You are surrounded by high, impenetrable walls; the walls are solid and thick and they protect you.

✧ In your mind, visualise a huge oak tree with enormous branches that reach out to the sky. The roots of the tree are strong and they grow deep, deep into the Earth. Allow the tree and yourself to become one as your mind allows these roots to spread out far and further, down, down, connecting as one with the planet.

✧ Feel and sense the life force of nature and the planet flowing up through these roots and filling you with strength and vigour. You feel invincible and untouchable.

✧ Look up and see the sun blazing in a blue sky overhead. Sense the energy and heat of the sun filling your solar plexus, below your ribs. Fill yourself with strong golden light as the sun's powerful energies fill you and spread through your entire body.

✧ Each breath brings in more and more strength and courage. Your mind is now filled with the power of this burning golden light and you let all negative and anxious thoughts burn up and dissolve.

✧ Your entire being is consumed with strength and golden light. You are strong, stable and totally in the present moment.

When fear runs out of control it can turn into paranoia, which means there is no logical substance to your fear and your anxieties take over and control your life. So work on quelling even minimal levels of anxiety. Once you get the first signs of butterflies in your stomach, once you feel unstable, once you sense a fluttering in your heart centre or feel your physical heart beating fast, get working on the exercises for stress and make sure you are in control.

'Your personal power is your strength - dig deep and stand strong.'

PARANOIA

When Gill Bailey, my editor at Piatkus, first contacted me to consider this book I was in the middle of a family crisis. My stepson, Tony, was becoming more and more disturbed by articles he was finding on the internet. He had read numerous pieces that persuaded him not only that his own life was under threat but, even more frightening, that his daughter's life too was in dire danger. He was convinced that we were under threat from secret societies that were plotting to take control of the world by destroying many of us and bringing the world's population down to a manageable size. Daily he came to me with 'proof'; he showed me videos and articles that included photos of concentration camps in America and transcripts of meetings between the most powerful and richest people on Earth conspiring to take over our lives, limit our movement and kill those who protested. I could see why he was impressed with these articles and videos, for they were all based on some level of fact, but with their use of second-hand narrative and exaggeration many of them had become, quite honestly, outrageous.

Tony was going through a difficult phase of his life and these stories fed his fears and anxieties, so that he fell into a state of paranoia. He couldn't sleep and, bless him, he ended up suffering a major psychotic attack, spending some time in hospital as a result. His daughter was distraught as her father swung between periods when he no longer recognised her and terror that she would be killed. As a result I understand how very important it is that we all keep strong when we read the media, that we understand that there are people in the world who deliberately want to destabilise us or make money from selling rumours and hype. The guidance and exercises in this book are focused on giving you back control of your will and your thoughts, on bringing you back to your natural sense of intuition and wisdom to know what is the truth, and on reconnecting you to your courage and inner strength to withstand the fears and to see everything, hear everything and value everything through the eyes and clarity of your own power.

'Other people's fears do not have to be yours.'

WHAT YOU CAN DO ABOUT STORIES IN THE MEDIA

If you find yourself caught up in a quandary as to whether you are reading or hearing myth or truth, what can you do? How do you know if what you read is true or not? Well, I would ask myself, does it matter? Does it really make any difference to your daily life? Can you do anything about it? If you can, then get into action and check it out. If not, let it go. Don't hold your fears but share them with your friends and close ones. The more you hold on to your fears the greater they will grow, and then your fears will get out of control. That is what paranoia is – out-of-control fears. Here is a checklist to follow if you find yourself in this situation:

✧ Ask yourself, is the matter that important? Who will it affect? This will prevent you from sliding into the morass of complex myths and conspiracies that, in all honesty, are not important in the greater scheme of things.

✧ Ask yourself, is this issue worthy of your fear and attention? It's entirely up to you if you want to spend your time on the internet investigating such issues, but wouldn't you be better spending your time helping out at the local charity shop? One route will bring you into a weakened and possibly paranoid state, while the other will fulfil you and make your stronger. It's your choice.

✧ If you feel the issue **is** worthy of your time, then contact your MP, write letters to newspapers, join action groups and keep nagging away until the truth is uncovered. Ask for details, ask for reports and find out what the experts are saying.

✧ When you read articles or hear about conspiracies, use common sense. Disregard the words of extremists who enjoy exaggerating and distorting the truth for the buzz and excitement of stirring up a storm. Better to read reports from the broadsheets with credible reporting rather than from some obscure website.

✧ If you have an anxious personality, keep away from the internet and minimise your exposure to the sort of news-papers, websites and magazines that revel in intrigue.

✧ Find people in authority or in your community that you can trust and ask their opinion.

✧ Keep working on the exercises in this chapter that will help you be strong when stress and fear starts to affect you.

Ultimately you are aiming to become at peace with your-self and focus on those things in your life that you can manage and control, while letting go of those that have a negative influence on you. The following prayer says it all:

Lord give me the SERENITY to accept the things I cannot change
The COURAGE to change the things I can
The WISDOM to know the difference

Remember this when you feel yourself sucked into a fear not of your own making.

'Be strong in your truth, your courage and your wisdom.'

All the work you are doing to build up your personal power will assist you in your intention to overcome your fears. You will find that as your solar energy grows, so you are less likely to succumb to your fears.

UNFINISHED BUSINESS – THE PROCESS OF EXPERIENCE

All changes to the way you are, to the way you perceive yourself and to your world require intention, determination, hard work and above all courage, especially when it comes to facing the things you fear the most. It's important to understand that you are making these changes not because there is anything wrong with you but rather to make you happier, stronger and more empowered. Your negative beliefs, fears, anxieties and emotional pain are actually the result of life experiences that are part of your journey.

Everyone has to experience loss, low self-worth, jealousy, etc., as well as arrogance, cold-heartedness and other negative traits that are on the opposite end of the behaviour and personality spectrum. What you don't want to do is wallow in these negative states. You know that self-acceptance, love, compassion and living joyfully works best, but it's impossible to get there without the wisdom that comes from experiencing and understanding all the challenges that life can throw at you. Whether the experiences occur from your choice or not, they are still invaluable for your growth. First, you need to identify the old emotions and attachments you have collected. Then we will look at how you can release or minimise their effects on your power and your ability to live life fully.

WHAT ARE YOUR OWN ISSUES?

Take a few moments to contemplate your own situation. This next exercise will need a truthful look at your issues, those situations that trouble you the most, old emotions that you hold and attitudes that you know cause you problems with others. In other words, look for the buttons that set you off into anger, self-pity, grief or any other negative state. You might like to do this with someone who knows you well, as you may be tempted to delude yourself. Your nearest and dearest may have a clearer insight into your hot spots and even their causes.

Exercise: What are your saboteurs?

Ask yourself the following questions. Take time and write down what you discover in your journal:

✦ What makes me angry?

✦ Do I hold any bitterness, resentment or anger about anything that has happened in my past?

✦ Do I accept myself totally or am I self-critical?

✦ What makes me anxious?

✦ Do I have any phobias?

✦ Do I avoid groups or large gatherings?

✦ Do I have high or low self-esteem?

✦ Do I have confidence?

✧ Do I have any regrets?

✧ Do I suffer from guilt about anything I have done or not done in the past or am doing now?

✧ Do I see myself as a victim or a victor?

✧ Do I get bullied or dominated easily at home or work?

✧ Do any members of my family or work colleagues frighten or intimidate me?

✧ How easily do I roll over and submit to another person's beliefs, ideas or control?

✧ Am I a controller?

✧ Am I a perfectionist?

As you answer these questions you will find the attitudes, traits and scars that act as blocks and saboteurs to your inner power and lower your energy vibrations, bringing you down and far away from your goal state of joy and vitality.

Old, hidden and suppressed emotions are caused by the unfinished process of learning life's lessons. Let's next look at this process, and then we can work on some of the emotions and attitudes you may still be struggling with.

THE PROCESS OF EXPERIENCE: HOW WE GROW SPIRITUALLY, MENTALLY AND EMOTIONALLY

The process of learning and growing follows a pattern and it's important to let it follow its full course.

Step 1: Something bad or seemingly bad happens. You are traumatised and often go into shock. If the event or situation is not too serious, you may just feel set back.

Step 2: You feel like a victim, that something or someone is to blame for causing what has happened – it may be yourself you blame.

Step 3: You become emotional. It's essential that you let the emotions flow and go, otherwise they will become part of you and you may begin to develop habits, personality traits and behaviour to mask them. These will then work against you and the emotions that are suppressed and bottled up underneath will act like poison on you mentally, emotionally, spiritually and physically.

Step 4: Once you have released the emotion, let it 'flow and go', you can gain clarity; you can begin to understand why you had the experience and what you can learn from it, no matter how painful it has been.

Step 5: The understanding of the lesson learned will turn into growth and strength, becoming wisdom that will guide you through similar situations in the future or help you avoid the cause of the experience. If you do not reach this stage, you will be guided back into similar experiences over and over again till you do 'get it'.

Unfortunately, most people get stuck at the emotional stage. They get attached and hold on to the emotions rather than letting them 'flow and go' and moving on to the stages of understanding and acquiring wisdom from the experience.

FER
GUILT
OLD MEMORIES
UNFINISHED BUSINESS
SELF-DOUBT,
ETC.

Hiding your power behind your saboteurs

EMOTIONS THAT DISEMPOWER

ANGER

Although it's perfectly OK to become angry when you have had a bad experience, anger is a strong and corrosive emotion if it's left unresolved for long. Over time it can damage your health. It will also confuse your thinking – people seeing the world through the eyes of anger are irrational, and when you are irrational you are coming from a place of weakness rather than a place of power. Use anger as an indicator that there is something wrong deep down, some unfinished business that needs resolving. To help you achieve resolution, identify the triggers for your anger – your family and or partner will probably be quite smart at finding these. I am sure they will tell you what sets you off on your high horse! Seek out the fear or pain that is lurking beneath your outrage. Your trigger could be intolerance, being ignored or disrespected, fear of loss of control or impotency, being criticised or a sense of being let down by yourself or others. Next you need to work on this and the cause, but don't be critical of yourself as the cause will be a past experience.

What you can do about anger

First of all, find the cause. Keep a diary for a month and make a note whenever you lose your temper, including what triggered the outburst. Write down all your feelings about the situation. After a month you will start to see a pattern.

Next, make a plan. Write down what you feel would ease your anger. Recognising it and making a plan will start to solve your problem.

Then you will need to find a way to express your disgust, your annoyance and let out all destructive feelings in a way that won't harm yourself or another person. Beat a pillow; shout out your feelings when no one is around; write your feelings down and burn them; exercise vigorously. Or try yoga, which is a great form of relaxation. There is a posture we use at my yoga sessions that reminds me of the New Zealand haka, where we push out our tongue and make our eyes bulge as we expel our breath. That's a great way of releasing bad feelings!

Finally, fight injustice. Anger is one extreme of a more manageable emotion – passion. Passion is a great motivator for change. When we are impassioned we are driven to change something, fight a cause or pursue a goal. Use your passion to fight any injustice that stirs you. Step up and offer a voice for the victims, or get help if there is any threat to your own safety.

'Release anger and all negative emotions to regain your energy and power'.

Meditation to heal anger

Follow this visualisation to release the bodily tension and disturbed emotions of anger. If you struggle to visualise or see with your inner sight, just hold the intention and know that the changes are occurring.

✧ Close your eyes and relax. Drop your shoulders and let go your frown as your face relaxes. Feel the tension leaving your body as you surrender to the intention of healing and releasing the anger within you.

✧ Focus on the part of your body where the feeling is strongest. It may be your heart or your solar plexus, or it might be a restriction in your throat.

✧ See it as a red ball of energy, it will be swirling and boiling like a hot ball of molten heat. With the knowledge that this is damaging you, hold the intention of releasing the heat and intensity of this energy.

✧ At your throat, see the ball of energy turn blue and spin into a perfect sphere of blue light – your throat relaxes and you can speak without anger now.

✧ At your heart, see the ball turn into a green sphere of light – your heart is releasing its pain and returns to a source of love.

✧ At your solar plexus, see the energy of temper and anger turn into an orange ball of light as it becomes once again your centre of strength and will, calm and strong. See the anger turn into passion and the source of action.

✧ Let this calming energy now flow through your entire body. Relax and unclasp your hands and feet, move through the muscles in your shoulders and back, letting go all tension.

REGRET

Regret is an emotion that can become a huge burden. It is debilitating and weakening and will take you back to the past, away from experiencing fully the life you are living right now. Do you ever say, 'What if', or 'If only', or my *bête noire* 'I should have'? Whenever you indulge in the sentiment of regret, you are sabotaging your power. That sounds harsh, but it's true.

What you can do about regret

Do you blame yourself for things that you didn't do? Do you keep looking into the past thinking, 'I should have done this' or 'if only I had done that'? If so, try to be less hard on yourself and remember that the person who made a choice ten years ago was less mature, less aware than you are today. Of course, with hindsight, there will always be different paths you would have walked if you'd known how they would turn out. When you are on a journey you have to make choices about routes, paths, diversions all the time. You make the best choice that you can with the information, understanding and wisdom available at that time. When you are travelling you are learning and acquiring knowledge and experience – all of which are positive in the bigger picture, even if they cause you grief and pain. How does a toddler learn balance, how does a child learn what heat feels like? Simply by trying and testing the world around them. So, don't regret the paths you have walked, don't regret the choices you have made. But look at the outcomes and learn from your mistakes, errors and poor calls. If you have hurt others with your actions in the past, take the lesson and use the experience to treat people better in the future.

So take one last look at the past, evaluate what you can take from the experience, learn your lessons and move on.

If you haven't learnt your lesson you will repeat the mistake again and again until you do learn. For this is the law of life. One of the prime reasons you are here on Earth is to learn and, from your lessons, to grow.

Exercise: Letting go of the regret of hurting someone

Use this exercise if you have hurt someone or missed an opportunity to show love or respect to someone, whether alive or dead.

✧ If the person is alive, simply ask for forgiveness. You may be surprised how pleased they will be to let go the blame they carry against you – that is, if they blame you at all. So often we build things up in our minds that actually are not such an issue.

✧ If the person is no longer around, follow these simple steps to communicate and release any regret:

   ✧ Find a quiet space and write a letter to that person. Express your regrets or your love, or both. Use this opportunity to share any emotions that you didn't get to share previously.

   ✧ If you feel that you have upset them in some way you can ask them to forgive you.

   ✧ Make a ceremony of lighting and burning the letter.

   ✧ As the letter burns know that the energies of the words and sentiments will pass your message into spirit.

   ✧ Hold the intention of releasing the burden of your past and to confirm this say out loud, 'I release and let go all regrets and step forward without the burden of the past'.

> When we do this exercise in workshops I feel the energies of love and remorse flowing away to the spirit energy of the person involved – it's very powerful, and very liberating for you too.

BLAMING OTHERS

Now we come to another negative attitude – blame. I introduced this subject in Chapter 1 in the sense of claiming self-responsibility, but it is an important aspect of being in your personal power, so I want to take a further look now at how it can make you a victim. Blaming others for your financial, physical or emotional state and for your misfortunes can take you straight into the state of being a *victim*. This will disempower you big time. It makes you weak and vulnerable and it gives control to your persecutor. The world is full of refugee camps, prisons and hospitals filled with innocents who are truly victims of the callous acts of power seekers, so unless you are a true victim of severe injustice then look beyond the actions of others and start to see your life from a positive perspective. You can use the exercise for positive thinking in Chapter 1 (see page 48) to help you move from a negative to a positive viewpoint.

'A victim sits in the shadows of life - forgive and step into the light.'

Case study: The Power of You to be self-responsible

Peter, heading for forty, perceives every aspect of his life through a haze of blame and considers himself a victim. He believes his parents have ruined his life. He believes their attitudes affected him negatively in his childhood and he holds on to that belief rigorously. As a result he has an unhappy, lacklustre life, none of his ambitions have been realised and his constant companion is misery.

Megan has spent her life looking for and finding everything that pleases, uplifts and encourages her. She accepts her parents were not perfect and understands that they have their own issues. Consequently, she has lived a happy life filled with love and great experiences. Peter and Megan are brother and sister with the same childhood experiences, but with different perceptions. The difference is that one blames other people and remains the victim, while the other has left behind the negative, taken the positive, moved on and made the best of her life.

What you can do about blaming others

If you are a genuine victim there is only way forward, and that is to get some form of resolution and then take back whatever you can from life and move forward. You need action to give you your strength back. So fight for justice, campaign for parity and get others to help you. Blame in itself is a negative state and will not bring strength, peace and joy. As we have seen from Nelson Mandela and the Dalai Lama, both men who have been through horrendous persecution and great loss, it is possible to regroup and move on. They are not burnt up with thoughts of revenge; they have not seen themselves at any time as victims. They have used their experiences to make themselves stronger and have gone on to inspire others.

Whatever pain or persecution others have put you through, try to let go of the past with forgiveness. It may be helpful to realise that most people who hurt others are themselves struggling with some inner, unresolved pain. Mostly people act with thoughtlessness rather than deliberate malice. Those who deliberately hurt others are coming from fear, pain and a lack of the understanding or experience of love.

Claim your life and your happiness as being in your control and your own responsibility. Make plans for how you will use the skills, the benefits and the opportunities you have to improve your life. Resolve to let go any signs or attitudes that encourage you to be the victim and think of yourself as a survivor.

'A victim is controlled by the actions of others. A victor takes that control back.'

Resolution not revenge

Resolution through finding justice is a positive route, while revenge is negative and destructive for all involved. When you deliberately hurt someone because they hurt you, the battle for power is prolonged and, like an argument, sends pain back and forth, disempowering both parties. As someone once said, when we hold a grudge we drink the poison and hope the other person dies. Bitterness, resentment and blame are toxic and can eventually even be physically harmful. The antidote for injustice is to do everything in your power to achieve a resolution, to get fair play, and then to move on with forgiveness or acceptance.

GUILT

Guilt is a heavy burden to carry and it can destroy lives. The uncomfortable feeling of guilt works as our self-punishment, and keeps us in line in terms of living and treating ourselves and others with love and compassion and living ethically. It is the action of the spiritual law of karma, the cause and effect of our actions. The pain of it shows you that you have either stepped out of the positive state of love and acted through fear, jealousy, hate or other negative state, or you have given yourself an opportunity to understand what it feels like to do something that hurts another human being. For example, if you hurt or kill someone through careless driving then you will have a huge burden to carry, but you will learn humility and compassion for your victim and painfully gain understanding of the law of karma.

'Guilt can take your power - find resolution, forgive yourself and move on'.

What you can do about guilt

Once you have carried and suffered the pain of guilt for some time, you need to look at how you can release it, for you cannot move on to the steps of understanding and wisdom if you do not release the emotion. You may find that you are drawn to 'give something back', either to the individual or to those that represent the damage you have done. Spiritually this is seen as a repayment of karmic debt, an act of service, an offering to an individual or society. It will help you to release the guilt which often sits in the pit of your stomach or feels like an icy grasp around your heart centre – as one person described it to me, 'I feel as though I have a fist in my chest.' So, if you are suffering from guilt, choose a route that will help you and others: for example, you can give money or time to charity, help friends and neighbours or work with environmental support organisations. Later in this book I will give many examples of how you can offer service to the community or individuals, and there is a list of websites for volunteers in the appendix.

Case study: The Power of You to forgive yourself

When Marina came to see me she was overloaded with guilt. She had had a dispute with her father and his wife some years before over property that they had built on her land. When her father died, she rented a place for her stepmother rather than give her money in compensation for the house. She told me this had caused huge schisms in her family and her stepmother's children were ostracising her. She had sleepless nights worrying about what she had done. She wasn't in a position to put the situation right – or felt unable to do so – and looked for a way to resolve the dispute and also the bad feelings she was experiencing.

I suggested she write to her stepmother explaining why she had acted the way she had; I also suggested she give some money to her, or if she didn't feel able to do that, to a charity for the homeless. She chose to do the latter and said she immediately felt hugely better, for now she had a plan and a way to move forward.

GRIEF AND ATTACHMENTS TO PEOPLE IN YOUR PAST

However well you organise your life, however spiritually you live your life, there will be times when disaster strikes, when you and those around you suffer. There will be times when you lose someone you love. Loss is inevitable, as is the natural feeling of grief that follows. The duration of your grieving will depend on how intense was your love of the one you lost. Grieving is a natural healing process, and it's a pity that in Western societies we don't follow the positive example of Middle Eastern, African and Asian cultures who allow themselves to scream, shout and wail out their feelings at funerals.

What you can do about grief

Grief and tears are unavoidable and are positive indicators that you are in touch with your feelings, that you feel love. You may suppress your grief but it will still exist. Any emotions you feel as a result of the loss of a loved one must be allowed to flow. Always let it out. Please don't be a martyr, don't feel you have to hold in your emotions for the sake of others, don't feel embarrassed to cry. Both men and women need to let inner pain be expressed, otherwise they suffer nightmares, depression, anger and physical problems.

As with letting go of blame, writing to someone who has passed on can be extremely therapeutic and can help you to let go some aspects of your grief. One of the most hurtful aspects of losing someone is your inability to speak and communicate with them any longer. Although it may seem strange or difficult to grasp, your loved one has moved on into spirit – their physical body may no longer be functioning but their soul energy certainly is. Although it cannot be seen, it is still within the dimensions of the universe and is connected to us through the universal energies of which we are all part. So if you speak or write to your loved one, they will understand what you are saying. Psychics and mediums access this connection through their third-eye chakra energy. You may not be able to hear any messages back simply because you have not developed that aspect of yourself, but they will most definitely be able to hear you. It can therefore be very helpful to write a letter expressing everything that you feel and were unable to say, or even the things you want to share now.

Attachments

Attachments between yourself and another can also be the source of problems. When you are in a close relationship your thought energy, as streams of consciousness, flows between the two of you, creating energy cords of attachment. In love songs these are called heart strings, as they link emotional heart to heart. Long after the person has gone, either through choice or death, you may still be connected by these cords of attachment. This can make it difficult to find a new partner, for while your heart is engaged with one person you will find it hard to create any deep and meaningful relationship with another. You will not be free; you will be limited and closed off. This also applies to situations of mistreatment and abuse that you have experienced in the past and which still bother you. Every thought directed over your shoulder holds you back.

Fond and loving memories about your loved ones who have passed on are your comfort and are invaluable to you, but if you yearn and hunger for that which you no longer have, then you are definitely not able to live your life to the fullest.

'Living in the past will take your power, living in the present empowers you.'

To allow you to move forward without the pull of the past you will need to release any attachments you have to the situations and people you wish to leave behind. The next exercise has proved to be an effective way to focus on this release. We looked at letting go our attachments to fear earlier; here is another way you can release yourself and move on.

Exercise: Releasing attachments

List all the people that you are unable to release from your life, heart and mind, whether through good or harmful connections. Then follow this visualisation to help you let go:

✧ Visualise that you are holding a number of strings attached to helium balloons that float in the air above you. Each balloon has the name of someone or a situation you wish to release.

✧ One by one let the balloons go, see them float off into the sky.

✧ Say your farewells to them as they float away and out of sight. You have empowered yourself and them with freedom.

✧ Say out loud ten times: 'I am free of all attachments that do not serve me and I am free.'

LOW SELF-ESTEEM AND CONFIDENCE

When you are not fully in your power you may suffer from a very fragile sense of self and your self-esteem can be destroyed or dented very easily. It can take just one word of criticism or one rejection to cast you into self-doubt. If you have been surrounded by people who have criticised you continuously, your confidence will also be severely affected.

As your confidence drops, you will withdraw and be scared to speak out and share your thoughts and feelings. You will start to limit your life and you will step out of your power. In a perfect world, everyone would feel happy and relaxed about speaking their mind and feelings without fear of being judged. But until we reach that wonderful time, you need to understand the effects of judgement, move towards self-acceptance (as we saw in Chapter 1) and find ways that you can manage other people's critical attitudes.

What you can do about low self-esteem

If you beat yourself up when you do not meet your own exacting demands, or are unsatisfied with your achievements, or if you keep expecting to be better, more proficient, more successful and never find anything you do good enough, you must ask yourself why. Are you frightened of being found lacking in some way? A much bolder and courageous way to live is to be accepting of yourself, to be less critical and forgive your own mistakes. Self-torment is destructive, and when you have low self-esteem you are easily overwhelmed by all the negative forces you encounter in your life. If you have been criticised and put down, remember that your true value is within and nobody can touch that. Your true self is still love – everything else is a distortion of your energies and your perception of yourself. We have talked about service and how taking up causes, helping others and speaking up can clear guilt. Well, it can also help you improve your self-image and value. On the next page is an exercise to assist you reclaim your confidence.

Get a friend or partner to list all those things she or he likes about you, and say why they chose you as a friend. Stick the list in your journal, on your mirror or on the fridge to remind you every day of your good points.

'Loving yourself and expressing your feelings are acts of empowerment.'

To help you express your feelings, practise the following exercise with a friend or partner. Sit with them and tell them everything you feel, your likes and dislikes.

Exercise to regain self-worth

In your journal, write down what you think would help you like yourself, trust yourself or respect yourself. Make that an action plan. List all your strengths and attributes – consider the following:

✧ What personal powers do you have that you do not utilise? Are you a leader, are you courageous, can you teach, etc.?

✧ What are your personal qualities? Are you kind, gentle, determined, focused, good with animals or children? Do you have patience with the elderly, do you listen to other people's problems? And so on.

✧ What were you good at when you were at school that you haven't revisited and made use of? Do you have any musical or creative talents that you could develop?

AVOIDING LIFE

There is a syndrome called Avoidant Personality Disorder, which is characterised by feelings of inadequacy, extreme sensitivity to negative evaluation and avoidance of social interaction. This behavioural pattern can develop from self-criticism, intolerance of self and low self-esteem. Sufferers believe they will be ridiculed, humiliated and rejected. Years ago we would have probably just described the person as shy, but it is a much more extreme case. There are, of course, variables and degrees of avoidance, but all are negative and disempowering. The fear can limit your life and prevent you from realising your dreams.

Case study: The Power of You with courage

I have a client who lived in a state of anxiety and feared social interaction so much that she couldn't leave her house and had no outside active life with her husband and children. Her mother's rejection and critical attitudes towards her when she was young were the underlying cause. She and I have been working together with her problem for the last two years; she is now able to take her children out in the car and is beginning to function normally. She has bravely worked through her fears and gradually, step by step, allowed herself to mix with people again. She has seen that her mother's behaviour was more about her and her own problems, that she had tried to empower herself by criticising and demeaning her daughter. She knows that it is her position to evaluate herself and to let no one adversely affect her with their opinions.

What you can do about avoidance

Whether you are avoiding social contact, close relationships and love or denying aspects of your life, you are limiting your life. All forms of avoidance weaken your core essence and inner strength and they need healing. They spoil your chances of being happy and living life to the full. The following exercise will help you take a good look at your life and enable you to go deep within so as to find the hidden dream that has never been fulfilled. Allow yourself time for this exercise – you may like to do it over a weekend or on a holiday. The more you put into it, the more powerful and effective it will be.

Exercise: The power of claiming your life

✧ Ask yourself whether you have any negative self-beliefs that may stop you achieving your goals. Are they your opinions or someone else's?

✧ Ask yourself what you can do to make yourself feel proud and happy with yourself. Set a plan for this and write it up in your journal with a start date. If you think you need therapy and help, write down your plan for getting this.

✧ Now look longer term. In your journal, write the heading 'Targets and Goals'. Start the rest of your life right now with a positive look at where you would like to be in six months, one year and five years. Include any dream, project or life plan that comes to mind.

✧ Meditate and see yourself living the dream. If you have difficulty visualising, then draw yourself acting out the dream. Stick men and simple graphics will do the job. See yourself stepping through any fears and limitations.

✧ Create a mantra or affirmation that enforces your action plan, for example, 'I am expanding my life', 'I step through my fears', 'I am achieving my dream step by step'.

✧ Write down the names of everyone you know who you can trust. See this as your core support group. Share your fears and anxieties with them and tell them of your plan to step through your fears. Ask them to help you.

Claiming your life is a positive and empowering aspir-
ation. Take one step at a time and gradually gather your
strength and courage to face people and life again. Be gentle
with yourself but also firm, because it is sad and distressing
to feel that you are missing out on the potential of life to
fill you with joy and happiness while you are hiding from
it through fear.

As you clear and release yourself from the mire of stag-
nant and stultified emotional energy from your past, you will
be setting yourself free to live your life in a more vibrant
and powerful way. You will also be better set up to manage
the threats and challenges that can affect you on a daily basis.

I will now lead you through the challenges you may meet
from those who share your life – family, friends and work
colleagues. We will look at ways that these challenges can
be mastered, avoided or overcome and how you can retain
your sense of empowerment.

THREE

Managing the Way Other People Affect You

We have seen how your own thoughts, attitudes and perceptions can seriously affect the way you feel and influence your sense of control over your life. We will now look further into the way you are affected by the mood, thoughts, actions and attitudes of those with whom you share your life. I will explain the impact both of unconsciously created negative energies and of those that are deliberately targeted towards you. We will see how you can stand strong and find your inner power to prevent your own spirits and health from going into freefall.

OTHER PEOPLE'S PERSONALITIES AND ATTITUDES

If you share your life with a person who is living in true, unconditional love and compassion, they make you feel loved, appreciated and supported. Unfortunately, the world

is a bit short on enlightened beings and many of the people
you mix with will have issues, emotional scars, unfinished
business and guilt. They may feel inadequate, unloved,
distrustful, angry and resentful. This is a shame, because their
issues will influence the way they treat you! Here are some
of the challenges you will face. I'll also explain how you
may be able to minimise their effects and manage to keep
yourself calm and centred.

MIRRORING

Before we look at other people and see how they affect you,
it is worth considering the reason they are in your life. The
people in your life will be mirroring you – if any of them
press your buttons, get you riled up and defensive, ask yourself why. If you find you have people in your life that irritate
and annoy you, check to see if there is any of their behaviour in your make-up. Why do they irritate you so much?

Mirroring is what we do when we draw towards us people
who have similar issues or personality traits, so that we can
learn more about ourselves.

Case study: Mirroring

*Two attractive, single women of about the same age decided to
move into a house together to share the upkeep and for company.
They had a lot in common – both were therapists and healers,
both were kind and loving and both were struggling financially.
Both women had lived on their own for much of their lives, and
maybe that's where the potential danger lay. Both were lovely
women, good fun and with strong personalities. But it turned
out to be the biggest mistake ever. Within six months fur was
flying and they had split up. Each of them had the same complaints*

about the other – not managing the housekeeping well, being too insular, finding the other's music, habits, etc. irritating. In fact they were too similar and didn't enjoy living with themselves! One of the two moved away; when she left the country she told me that the lesson had been a good one. She was more powerful, more in control when she was alone, making her own decisions and running her life her own way.

So just bear in mind that if you share your life with anybody with the following personality traits, it may pay to ask yourself why you have drawn them into your life and what lessons they are bringing for you. It may be to learn more about yourself, it may be to teach you to be strong and it may teach you tolerance, where to place your boundaries. It may just be a reflection of yourself.

'The powerful way is - be true to yourself.'

JEALOUSY

Insecurity and a sense of injustice causes jealousy, something you may encounter with your brothers and sisters or with colleagues at work. There doesn't have to be a valid cause – if someone perceives that you are getting better treatment, more love or special concessions, then they can become jealous. Being with an individual or a group of people who are jealous of you will affect your energy levels. You may feel a sense of anxiety, with symptoms such as butterflies in your stomach, and over time it will bring down your spirits and make you feel depressed. Visible signs may include spiteful comments, flirting with your friends and partner or trying to show you in a bad light.

If you can understand the basic insecurity that sits behind the jealousy it will help you to deal with it better. People who feel confident and happy with themselves and their situation will not feel jealous or unhappy about someone else's good fortune. You can protect yourself by insulating your energy field, which will enable you to minimise the effects of the negative energy. Later in this chapter I will give you a number of ways to do this.

There are also more positive things you can do to help. You can send love to the person. Love is the antidote to jealousy and all negative emotions. Love is high-vibration energy and its wavelengths will lift the low, heavy energy of insecurity and low self-esteem. It will also help the person to feel happier, and happy people make good companions.

You can be obviously kind and helpful. By showing kindness and friendship to the person you will create a bond between you. Jealousy often leads to gossip, which can spread the negativity. If you get closer to the person involved they are less likely to talk about you.

'Love is the antidote to all negativity.'

ANGER

Other people's anger needs to be handled carefully, otherwise it may brim over into violence. It is a power threat and when a person shows anger towards you it is intended, maybe unconsciously, to make you feel threatened and submissive, and to make you give your power away to the 'victor', who is then in control of you. Road rage is probably the most common manifestation of anger we will experience from a stranger. I actually feel sorry for someone who can get into such a tizzy because a driver in front of them is lost or confused, or who is not going as fast as they would like. So, how best to deal with someone who is angry?

What you can do about anger

First, don't retaliate or you will fuel the anger and a fight – either vocal or physical – will begin. Defuse the conflict by ignoring the first outburst; it is a test to measure your response.

When someone attacks you with their anger, visualise pulling down a shutter in front of you. This symbolically shields you from the onslaught and is a very effective way of minimising the energetic effects of the negative stream targeted at you. You can also imagine you have a shield that you hold up to stave off the attack.

Don't cower when someone verbally attacks you. Stand up strong – don't be aggressive, but be firm and show strength. If your heart is racing, as it probably will, it is an instinctive flight or fight reaction. Slow your pulse by breathing very slowly and deeply for a few moments. This will have the effect of calming you down, physically and emotionally.

Despite these measures, you will naturally feel upset when you have been attacked. Afterwards, away from the protagonist, let your feelings flow – in whatever way suits you!

DISTRUST AND INABILITY TO EXPRESS LOVE

It can be very upsetting if you are in a relationship where you feel the other person is just not committed to you or able to give you the love you expect. This may be because they have had a previous experience of rejection that has hurt them deeply. When we are hurt or discarded by someone we love, our heart is emotionally and energetically damaged – hence the expression 'a broken heart'. The natural response to this is to close down and shut the doors of our heart, or even to put up some form of barricade to prevent a further close encounter. It may be difficult for your partner to trust you, and you may be experiencing the effects of this in your relationship if you feel shut out. When you love someone, you naturally want them to commit too. If they cannot, you will feel rejected and shut out. What can you do in these circumstances?

What you can do about distrust

Sometimes things can be resolved with long chats and by sharing your expectations. You both need to have the same level of commitment for a relationship to work in the long term. Maybe your partner just doesn't want the responsibility of a long-term relationship, maybe he or she feels overwhelmed by your attention. You can only deal with these issues between you if you can get your partner to speak up.

If your partner has been hurt in love before, help them to open their heart and suggest therapies such as counselling and healing. Your love in itself may well be the trigger to bring back trust, but if the wounds go very deep more help may be needed.

Try to avoid seething and holding in your own resentments, for this will eventually result in an explosion that can permanently damage the relationship. You need to express your own feelings of being excluded and it's essential that you open the dialogue – your partner may never find the courage to do this.

If, over time, however, you find that one of you cannot fully commit, then you do not truly have a close relationship. Hard as it may sound, it would be best to move on, otherwise you will feel disappointed as your expectations are dashed.

'Share your feelings, unexpressed emotions are disempowering.'

UNFAITHFULNESS

It's painful to be rejected, put second or deceived. When a partner is unfaithful it will naturally affect your confidence and self-esteem. You will feel out of control of your relationship, vulnerable and disrespected. As with all bad behaviour that affects you, you have the right to speak up and express your feelings. Some people just don't handle responsibility and commitment well. Some are emotionally immature, short on empathy or unable to understand the effects of their behaviour on others, some are callous or actually unable to love and commit fully. All these difficulties may be the result of some trauma they experienced earlier in their life, but you have to be sure that their problems don't ruin your own life.

If your partner or lover is regularly unfaithful, you have a number of choices.

What you can do about unfaithfulness

First, weigh up whether your partner will change. It may help if you understand why they act the way they do. Decide either to tolerate their behaviour or be prepared to end the relationship; you don't want to be bringing the matter up in every argument in perpetuity.

'Making a choice and having a plan of action will empower you.'

If your partner is a serial offender you do not have a close, balanced relationship anyway and you are obviously not respected. You may, however, want to forgive a one-off situation if all other aspects of your relationship are good. I know many people who have brilliant marriages that have survived one blip, and I know others who are lonely and regretting a hasty divorce.

Whatever choice you make, though, let it be your own, not your mother's or your friend's. They do not have to live with the consequences – you do.

NEEDINESS

Do you know someone who calls you up constantly seeking your opinion, bewailing their problems or asking for help? Behaviour like this can be exhausting! They may act this way because they are insecure and unable to cope with life. Energetically they will be hooking in and sucking your energy, leaving you drained. If they rely on you too much, you will also feel the burden of their expectations and your own sense of duty and responsibility. The illustration below shows how it affects your energy field.

It can be easy to fall into the trap of feeling you are responsible for making all those close to you happy and fixing their problems. If you take over their lives, though, they will become more and more dependent and less empow-

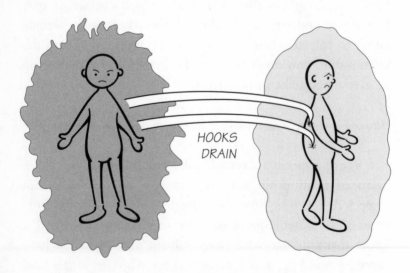

Hooks from a needy person drain your energy

ered. It is also impossible to *make* a person happy. You can change their surroundings and you can treat them well; you can give advice and assistance. But if they are negative or living the life of a victim, you will not be able to change that. So make sure your boundaries are strong. There are several ways you can do this.

What you can do about neediness

First, say 'no' when you have given enough. This will help you to create strong energy boundaries. Sense when you are tired and need to support yourself, and when your involvement is limiting the other person's growth. Try to understand whether other people are acting out of real need or selfishness.

'Learning when to say "no" is empowering.'

You should also take steps to protect yourself. You can protect your own energies from others demanding ones by imagining yourself putting on a cloak that protects your back,

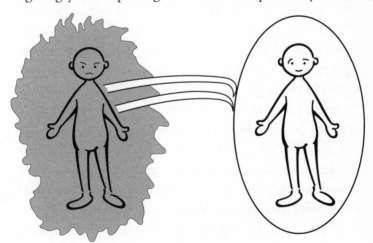

**WITH STRONG BOUNDARIES YOUR
ENERGY FIELD STAYS STRONG**

which is where needy hooks can lodge. And make sure you take time out and away – if you do not, you will burn out and get sick.

DEPRESSION, ANXIETY AND PESSIMISM

A person who sees life through a glass darkly can also be very tiring to have around. If others constantly talk of the negative and bad things that are happening in the world and expect the worst all the time, you will struggle to keep your own thoughts and expectations positive.

Case study: The Power of You to uplift your life through positivity

Mel lives with a man whose cup is always half empty. Even when something good happens, he will say, 'That won't last' or 'Wait and see, it won't be as good as you think.' He is frightened of hoping for something good in case it doesn't happen, and he fears the worst. Mel is the opposite and is optimistic all the time. She sees the best in people and expects good outcomes. She manages their relationship well by not allowing his pessimism to affect her. If he doesn't want to take up invitations to parties, she goes alone. She says, 'I will not let him destroy my happiness, I will continue to live my life and I refuse to be miserable' – the very best way to deal with this situation. She also sees the good in her husband and focuses on that, rather than letting his negativity affect her and their relationship. Actually he is suffering from depression and would benefit from treatment, but he adamantly refuses it. So she has no other recourse but to get on with her life, which she is doing most successfully.

What you can do about negativity and pessimism

If you share your life with a pessimist, there are a number of things you can do to clear negative energy and strengthen your own positivity:

✧ Visualise yourself stepping into an egg. This egg has thick walls and nobody's negative energies or emotions can get through them to affect you.

✧ Ensure you keep your own energy levels up – speak, think and act positively yourself. Keep reminding yourself of the good things in your life, the best aspects of your partner, your gifts and strength.

✧ Use positive affirmations to remind you that you are in charge of your happiness, for example, 'I am strong and self-sufficient', 'I can make my own happiness'.

✧ Get out and about with friends so that you have a break and a change of scene.

✧ Make your own life as full and happy as you can. Follow pursuits that please you.

✧ Spray the rooms of your house, especially those where the person sits regularly, with a cleansing spray. I have created one called Cleansing and Clearing which I use in my healing room – it effectively disperses any negative energy fields. You can use Peppermint, Sage, Frankincense or Sandalwood, either in a spray or as incense.

✧ Crystals in the room will clear negative energy. Clean them once a week by soaking in water with sea salt, then recharge their energies by putting them in the sun or moonlight.

✧ Stand in the centre of the room and allow your sun energy, your solar plexus energy, to fill the room. Call in the strength of the Solar Logos to fill the room with golden light, then fill the room with love by visualising love flowing from your heart centre. See the love as beams of pink light.

'The person best suited to making you happy is yourself.'

SELFISHNESS

Me, me, me. This behaviour pattern and attitude is very similar to neediness. But whereas the person who is needy may actually need some support and advice, the selfish person has a problem realising that there are other people outside of their world who also have needs and feelings. Children act like this, and teenagers too – in fact they excel in this behaviour!

Selfishness is a sign that the person hasn't evolved beyond childhood. Either those around them are doing everything for them and giving them everything they desire, or they have been let down by people and have decided to look out only for themselves. So how can you manage other people's selfishness?

What you can do about selfishness
If you share your life with a selfish person, take care not to feed their belief that they are more important than others by doing everything for them. This is a danger mothers can fall into, especially with their sons.

Express your feelings – show the person how their actions affect you. If they live in a bubble they may not recognise or empathise with how you are affected. But make sure to avoid shouting and castigating – it just makes your energies more depressed and lowers the energy of the home or workplace.

Encourage independence by rewarding any personal support and self-responsibility. If it is a family member who is acting selfishly, ask them to help you. It is harder to turn down a direct request. Then thank them.

If there is no change, if possible, move on. Instead surround yourself with people who are kind and giving.

UNKINDNESS AND CRUELTY

These are attitudes you may come across at home, in the workplace or from strangers in the street. In close relationships it's not uncommon to find that one partner tries to dominate the other through mind games, manipulation by guilt and full-on cruelty. The problem is that what may start as a mild bossiness or protectionism can quickly escalate into full-scale abuse – mental, emotional and physical.

Case study: The Power of You to be free

Susan was abused by her first husband. When she was asked why she hadn't left him earlier, she said, 'You become so totally afraid, you live in fear and then it seems that you have no options.' Initially she accepted his behaviour because she had been brought up in a family where domestic violence regularly took place. It was the normal way for couples to behave; she saw nothing strange in the fact that her husband beat her when she annoyed him! But she looked around and saw that this was actually not the norm, that other people had loving relationships without jealousy, possessiveness and violence. She realised that if she was to be happy, she had to be strong and find the courage to make that decisive step away. She realised that the only person who could change her life was herself. It was up to her to make things better – she deserved better and she was going to make it happen. One day she packed her bags and left. She still loved her husband and she was terrified of the future, but she knew that what she had was never going to make her happy. She found the strength and she made her move. Since that day her life has got better and better and she is now in a very loving and supportive relationship.

Do you suffer from controlling or abusive behaviour? Try communicating your feelings when your partner is in a more responsive mood and help your tormentor understand the effects of their behaviour. They may see their controlling ways as being protective and not realise how overpowering it can be; they may see their jealous rages as a sign of their love for you. If they have no compassion for your suffering, then move away from them – or report them, depending on your circumstances. The worst thing you can do is nothing, for that is tantamount to giving them permission to continue behaving badly. One way or another you have to find your inner strength – the strength we all have as an aspect of our personal power, our inner spirit – and stand up to cruelty wherever and whenever you come across it. If you are a witness, speak up. If you are a victim, act: report it, confront it or move away from it.

'The strength is within you - you just have to find it.'

Case study: The Power of You to protect yourself

A neighbourhood was suffering at the hands of a gang of young people who tormented the residents daily. Many of the community were elderly and disabled. Although they were obviously miserable with this treatment, they had a fighting spirit and were determined not to give in to the abuse. After numerous reports to the police and the council, nothing had changed, so they took the initiative and installed a number of cameras around their homes as a personal protection scheme. Every evening one particularly feisty middle-aged lady would stand at the end of the close, protecting her vulnerable neighbours. Well over sixty, she was an amazing role model of fighting spirit, a true spiritual warrior exhibiting strength and compassion.

Connect to your inner strength

When you connect to your inner power of strength, people can instinctively tell and they are far less likely to try to push you around, mentally or physically. I worked for some years with a computer manufacturing company and I had to travel to some very obscure parts of the world on my own. Often I was quite nervous of the situations that I found myself in – there were probably enough to fill another book! When I felt vulnerable I would draw myself up and feel myself growing stronger and larger – I took on the attitude 'Just don't mess with me, don't even dare.' I was treated with respect everywhere I went, from northern India and Pakistan to the depths of Africa. I had connected to my inner strength.

What you can do about unkindness and cruelty

When you are faced with abusive or cruel behaviour, know that whatever other people say to you, however they treat you and however desperate you feel, they cannot touch the inner you, your free spirit, your free will, the very essence of who you are. They cannot destroy the real YOU, for that is inviolate. In such situations, turn your focus away from your tormenters and their actions and concentrate on building up your inner strength. Turn the other cheek and let their words and insults fly over you – metaphorically *duck*.

Keep in mind that this is their unfinished business, their old wounds and troubles surfacing. Don't let them destroy you or sink to their level. And never let go the principles of love, kindness, generosity, fortitude, and all those other powerful aspects of the human spirit that are your core. When it gets overwhelming, go back into your heart as we did in 'Align with the power of love and step into your heart' exercise in Chapter 1. Remember who you are.

THE POWER OF YOU TO CHOOSE A PARTNER – WITH CARE

Negative and self-centred traits have a serious impact on close relationships. You cannot choose your parents and siblings, so you more or less have to do the best you can with those relationships, using tolerance or avoidance. Your work situations are a little more flexible – if you have a boss who upsets you, at least you have the choice of changing job. But our personal relationships, friends and lovers are all our own choice.

What do you look for in a relationship? Many of us click into a close relationship initially because we are attracted by looks, charisma, sexual desire and an indefinable feelgood factor. All of which are just fine, but you can save yourself a great deal of grief in the long run if you check, before you commit yourself, to see if the *person makes you feel good about yourself.* Self-esteem and confidence are easily bruised or shattered, so you do not want to live with someone who affects these. So remember the following:

✧ Make sure your relationship builds your self-esteem rather than destroys it.

✧ Take your happiness into a partnership rather than expect happiness from it.

✧ Have reasonable expectations rather than Mills and Boon dreams. Then you will start off with a realistic mindset and hopefully have less disappointments.

'Judge a relationship by how good the person makes you feel about yourself.'

The traits of behaviour and attitude we have looked at so far are fairly obvious to spot and we can react accordingly when we experience them, but there are other negative energies that we don't see. All negative attitudes towards you or around you are going to have some effect on you, whether you identify them or not, so we will now look more closely at why and how they affect us.

OTHER PEOPLE'S ENERGY FIELDS AND THOUGHTS

The atmosphere around you is filled with beams of energy. These come from many sources including radios, televisions, microwaves and GPS systems. I describe how these can affect you in my book *Healing Negative Energies* (see appendix). However, there are many other energy forces that you cannot see but which can also have a profound effect on your feelings and your wellbeing. Energy comes in a range of vibrations

– from the very highest, which is light, with positive and uplifting effects on the human energy field, to the negative, lowest and densest, which is toxic and detrimental to us physically and also adversely affects our feelings.

We are all sensitive to this unseen negativity, some more than others. Ask yourself the following:

✧ When you walk into a crowded room, does it have any effect on you?

✧ Do you know when someone is upset without them speaking?

✧ Do you feel uncomfortable if someone sits too close to you?

✧ Can you sense when there is someone looking at you?

✧ Have you ever intuited when someone you love is sick?

These are all signs of your sensitivity to the thoughts and energies of others. The people you meet and who share your life will have a full range of thoughts and attitudes that can affect you subconsciously: pessimism, fear, remorse, jealousy, insecurity and, on the positive side, love, joy and optimism. These thoughts attract each other and gather together to create clouds of massed energy that hang around them and the places they frequent. The atmosphere of your office or workplace will be affected by these clouds. After a party or celebration the atmosphere can be charged with the energies of fun and laughter, music and excitement, and stadiums, clubs and theatres are usually filled with the upbeat and positive energy of thrill and enjoyment.

'Positive thoughts and attitudes empower and uplift your energy field.'

PROTECTING YOURSELF FROM NEGATIVE ENERGIES

You will need to protect yourself from the negative effects of these dense energies. The most powerful form of protection is your own inner light and strength. As you become more empowered you will withstand the pressures of external negativity. As we saw in Chapter 2, your own issues, scars and negativity can be a magnet for bad luck, negative attitudes and abusive people, so the more work you do on yourself and the more positive you can be, the less likely you are to be seriously affected.

If you are unsure whether you are being affected by external or internal energy forces, you can use this simple technique: stand under a shower and let the water flow all over you. If you feel your energies change and if you can hold a positive thought, then the negativity comes from outside; if you feel the same as before then you are the cause of your own problem.

Here are some methods you can use to protect your energy: if you struggle to visualise, say the words to yourself and let your intention to protect yourself make it happen.

Violet flame. This visualisation is the one I use to clear and protect my energies when I am in a crowd or a hospital, on a plane or train. Visualise a violet (deep purple) flame burning up around you.

Pink and blue orbs. Good for protecting a number of people. I use this in workshops and when healing. Visualise pink orbs or love around each person, including yourself, and a blue orb of light around your home.

Protective mirror. If you feel that someone is constantly sending negative energies against you, this is a good protection. Visualise a cone made of a mirror that surrounds you at an

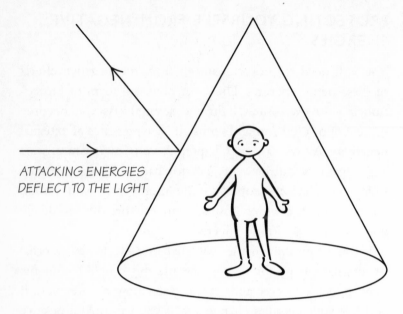

ATTACKING ENERGIES
DEFLECT TO THE LIGHT

Mirror cone protection – outer surface is a mirror

angle of 45 degrees (see the illustration above), reflecting any negativity up into the sky.

Four trees. This has worked well for me when I have been bothered by a difficult elemental energy. See four large trees in a square around you. See golden chains wrapped around the trees and a white light flowing down around you.

Archangel Michael. Michael is the most powerful Angel of Protection. Angels will always come when called and angelic energies are pure and light. His strength is reassuring and the perfect foil against psychic attack. Say 'I call in the presence of Archangel Michael to protect me and keep me safe.' Repeat three more times.

Protection symbol. This was given to me by my spirit guides, the highly evolved spiritual beings that come to me with

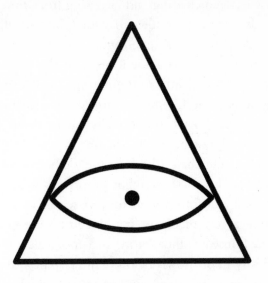

Protection symbol

guidance when I am in meditation. Draw the symbol above in the air over yourself. You can draw it on paper and put it in your car, under your bed or in your bag. I have had it crafted into silver jewellery – a pendant and earrings (see appendix for details).

Essential oils. There are powerful protective properties in certain plant extracts, such as Rosemary and Laurel. You can burn oils in your home or use a spray containing a blend. A Protection oil and Aura spray created from organic essential oils are available from Ripple (see appendix).

Crystals. Tourmaline, Obsidian and Red Agate are all good protective crystals to wear or keep around you. Cleanse them regularly in sea salt and water and re-energise in sun or moonlight. Even better, put them out in a thunderstorm.

Clearing space. Any space that gets contaminated by negative energies will need clearing and cleansing from time to time. If there has been any conflict in your home or office, then you can clear it by using essential oils such as Juniper, Peppermint or Sage. As I mentioned in the section about depression and pessimism, Ripple has a Cleansing and Clearing spray that is effective for space clearing. North American Indians have traditionally burnt dried sage and this works well, but be careful of fire alarms! Frankincense placed on burning charcoal is extremely efficient for clearing any space. Set the charcoal alight outside, as it will send off strong smoke and fumes itself until it settles to a hot glow. Then place a few pieces of frankincense on top and take around the house or office, letting the smoke clear the atmosphere. The symbol shown below will clear negativity. Draw it once and visualise it spinning in an anti-clockwise direction around the room, absorbing and transforming the energy – rather like PacMan!

You can also keep the energies of your home uplifted by playing bright music and displaying fresh flowers.

Finally, let's look at the deliberate use of energy to cause

Symbol to clear negativity

us discomfort, throw us off balance and in some, thankfully rare, cases cause physical and mental mayhem.

DELIBERATE ATTACKS – BLACK MAGIC, SPELLS AND CURSES

In the last fifteen years I have spent much of my time healing and working with people in Africa and the Far East, and my experiences there have dispelled any thoughts I might have had that there was no such thing as black magic. I have seen a woman turn black from the effects of a curse, seen the nails that a shaman took out of a man's leg, had my own legs turned to rubber by an angry *sangoma* (witch doctor) in South Africa, fought a dark spirit who had possessed a woman in Malaysia and come face to face with a witch doctor when clearing a spell. I have cleared curses from the highest of government officials and spells from the poorest of the poor. I have also learnt that light is stronger than darkness and that love is more powerful than hate.

Shamans and witch doctors are practised in the arts of manipulating and using energy either for good or evil, depending on their own integrity and ethics. They almost all work for money. Most of the cases of black magic I have come across overseas have been initiated by jealousy, sexual desires and the craving for power and money. A couple of years ago I cleared a curse from land in Zambia, but unfortunately, by doing this, I showed my power to the village *sangomas*. The next day, after a visit to a nearby village, I felt my legs turn to rubber and I almost collapsed. It took a couple of hours of meditation and prayers before my energy returned. It was a nasty experience but it taught me caution, especially where the dark arts are practised. It also taught me that the powers of love and giving are far stronger than the powers of greed, jealousy and self-interest.

'Love is the ultimate power.'

Certain people are more likely to be affected than others by the practice of the dark arts. Of course, if you live in a culture where black magic is prevalent then you are more exposed. In those cultures businessmen, politicians, police, judges and others in public office are often attacked. Spells, curses and magical potions are forceful energies that take control of people's minds, feelings and actions, but remember that you have access to unlimited positive energy through your inner strength and love, and this connects you to the limitless love and strength of the universe. The stronger you are the less likely you are to be affected. Healers will help clear curses by accessing the higher vibrations of love and light. I have done so in the past and the effects can be quite dramatic.

'The blend of strength and love is the most powerful force in the world.'

WHAT YOU CAN DO ABOUT NEGATIVE ENERGIES

In my book *Healing Negative Energies* I have shared ways of detecting and protecting yourself from unseen energies, either those radiated by other people or those deliberately projected towards you. So here I will just pinpoint a few symptoms to watch out for and ways you can protect yourself.

Am I cursed or being psychically attacked?

Very few people are ever affected by external energies to the point that it affects their life; mostly they are experiencing issues of their own that need resolving. If you do think you may have been cursed, or affected by a spell or some supernatural energy, then here are some indicators to look out for:

✧ You feel heavy and lack energy to the point of exhaustion.

✧ Your spirits are continuously low even though you work on positive thinking and positive attitudes.

✧ Bad luck dogs you at work, or with your finances or health. Every venture you step into fails despite the right support and planning.

✧ You are interrupted in the night and feel a presence, sometimes even feel you are being interfered with sexually.

✧ You feel compelled to be with someone whom you don't trust or even like, but still cannot drag yourself away.

✧ Your mind is full of thoughts that are not your own, or you hear voices telling you to do things that are not in your best interests or could harm other people.

✧ You feel the atmosphere around you dropping in temperature and you sense a spooky feeling.

The next exercise shows you what you can do if you feel you are cursed.

As you become stronger by healing your own issues, protecting your energy field, enhancing your power centre

Exercise: Clearing a curse

✧ First, visualise yourself surrounded by the violet flame of protection (just hold the intention that you are surrounded by the violet flame and are well protected if you find it difficult to visualise).

✧ Connect to a spiritual source of light such as Jesus, Kwan Yin, Archangel Michael or other spiritual master – or visualise the intense light of the sun and hold the intention of the light burning up all negativity that is affecting you.

✧ See yourself completely covered and filled with this light, transforming all energies to light.

✧ Affirm, 'I am filled with light and love and all that is not love is transformed to light.' Repeat three more times.

and focusing on positive thoughts and energy, you will be less and less affected by those around you. We'll next look at ways that you can enhance your power as you face the daily challenges of everyday living.

FOUR

Being Powerful in Your Daily Life and Work

Every day you have opportunities to develop and utilise your personal power. You have opportunities to be the best you can be in everything you do, no matter how small or seemingly mundane. You can focus on the moment, being totally present and enjoying and getting the best out of every second of your life. There are many challenges, though, that will endeavour to take you out of this ideal state, and you need to be aware of ways that you can hold your power when you come up against them. In this chapter we will see how we can manage our power when faced with issues of money, dealing with authority, bullies and crime – all situations that you may come up against in your daily life. We will also take a look at some of the roles that you may play – parent, carer, employer and so on; how you can be empowered in these roles and how you can effectively help others through them.

In recent years, not only have we experienced our own issues about money – usually the lack of it or overextending our credit – but also our governments have managed us into debt and the entire financial sector has fallen into disrepute.

Add to this the fact that 1.4 billion people live on less than
$1.25 a day – in other words, below the poverty line. This
means that a vast percentage of the world is disempowered
financially. So I will start with our relationship with money.

USING YOUR POWER TO DEAL WITH MONEY, LACK AND CREATING ABUNDANCE

Through my work and from my own experiences I have
discovered some interesting dynamics that occur with money.
Money is a form of energy, so your relationship towards it
will be affected by your own thoughts, fears and attitudes.
If you fear it, it will pass you by. If you respect it, you will
find it easier to acquire it. If you feel unable to support yourself and cope alone, then you will find yourself with difficulties
in supporting yourself financially as well. Self-esteem, confidence, self-respect, being lovable and respected are all aspects
of your relationship with yourself, and all will affect your
relationship with money – in fact, with the abundance of
everything, including good relationships, happiness and health.
As you work through your healing of the symptoms of past
problems and see yourself in a more positive light, so your
ability to attract money will improve.

When you feel that you are lacking, then you are disempowered, for lack is a weak and vulnerable position. If you
are totally lacking security and financial support, you drop
to the level of desperation and then you feel helpless – which
is, of course, the complete opposite of the satisfaction and
fulfilment you feel when you have all you need in life. Our
expectations may vary – what is a necessity for one may be
a luxury to another – but you need to manage your own

expectations of money and financial support. Either you must find ways to meet your expectations that suit you, or you must lower those expectations. We'll now look further into these issues of poverty, financial expectations and your relationship with money and wealth.

POVERTY CONSCIOUSNESS

This is an expression that is used frequently these days and I thought I should give you my understanding of what it means. It refers to a way of thinking, an expectation of how rich your life will be. It reflects your attitude to money, prosperity and abundance. If you have poverty consciousness it means you expect to be poor, you are programmed to be poor, you do not think you are worthy of anything else. There are entire communities and even countries where this is the norm.

'If you have the will you have the power to reach your dreams.'

However, as you know, some individuals from even the poorest of families rise above the heavy chains of lack and manage to achieve prosperity for themselves. They usually have the help of some Good Samaritan who crosses their path, but what is it that makes them stand out? What is it that attracts good fortune to them? I believe it's an attitude of inner belief and the personal power that I have described already. The force of this energy, fuelled by self-acceptance, hope and determination, will take an individual from a group believing in poverty and allow him or her to fly. As you work on healing your inner emotional and spiritual wounds and discover the good and valuable aspects of your-self, focusing on these above all else, so you will be able to shift the burden of the heavy energy that your culture, society, family, or even your own mind, has created for you.

'A person cannot be pulled out of poverty but they can be helped to lift themselves out.'

There are many rags-to-riches stories from all societies that can inspire us to throw off the limiting chains of poverty. In the UK we certainly have our share, but one that has become famous through his television show *The Apprentice* is that of Sir Alan Sugar, whose father was a tailor in the East End of London's garment industry. As a child Sir Alan lived in a council flat, yet he is now one of the richest men in the UK with an estimated wealth of £830 million. You probably know someone yourself who has worked their way from poverty to wealth. My own husband was born in a converted bus, the son of a fairground worker, and ended his career as the CEO of a large corporation. Such people show that when you have a dream, a goal and a strong inner desire and determination to reach it, you can reach that goal even if you were born in poverty or lack.

GIVE AND TAKE – THE DYNAMICS OF WEALTH

I have been through tough times in my life like everyone else, and I have struggled financially at times too. But one interesting spiritual truth I have found is that when you give wealth away without any expectation of reward, it will almost always come back to you. I find that whenever I give a dona-tion to charity or give money to help somebody, it flies back to me from another, often unexpected source. If I need funds for a project, I visualise the money I need coming in – and, lo and behold, it always works. Here is the method I use:

Meditation to attract prosperity and abundance

✧ Close your eyes, relax, drop your shoulders.

✧ See yourself surrounded by white light – know that you are protected and secure.

✧ Say 'I am open to receive abundance and prosperity'. See doors opening and golden coins showering down upon you.

✧ Acknowledge that the universe will always support you. See your heart centre opening to send love and support to all those that need it at this time.

✧ Visualise abundance flowing as gold coins towards those that you know are in need.

✧ Feel the balance of life as you receive and give – you and the universe are in complete harmony.

PRACTICAL STEPS TO MANAGE YOUR MONEY

The financial crisis left us feeling vulnerable and fearful. Here are a few ideas to help you feel stronger and more in control:

✧ Set up a regular savings scheme, so that you have some resources for a rainy day.

✧ Make sure you don't have all your financial eggs in one basket – diversify your investments, even if you only have a little money. Put some in the Post Office, some in a savings account, some into a property bond, and so on.

✧ Budget your money carefully and avoid overspending on credit cards.

✧ Take advice from an expert before exposing yourself financially to any venture or project.

GRATITUDE

Gratitude is a powerful energy and the feelings and sense of it can do much to make us feel full, satisfied and empowered. This is why even the poorest people in the world can be empowered. Even though their wealth and security may be minimal, their appreciation of what they have makes them strong. When you have the sense of being fulfilled and surrounded by the natural riches of life – children, the sun, nature and so on – then you step out of the weakness of lack and into strength.

It's worth spending some time to contemplate all the gifts you have, no matter how small, and look for things in your life to appreciate and feel grateful for. Give value to everything – yourself, your life, those that share your life, your material possessions and the money you have – however much or little that may be. Through gratitude you open yourself spiritually and then energy flows to and fro, naturally and easily, and you can share the bounties of life. As satisfaction, acceptance and gratitude spread around the world there will be less protectionism, less greed and less fear relating to poverty and lack.

'Gratitude and appreciation lift your spirits and bring abundance.'

SHOPPING

One aspect of daily life that we all have to experience is shopping. This can offer us an opportunity to use our personal powers, not only to get the best for ourselves and our families, but also to affect the wellbeing of those who work to bring the goods to our shops.

By your choices, your demands and product selection, you can influence the practices of large retailers and help those in the world who may be dominated and bullied by the large organisations that buy from farmers, small factories and miners. There has been a growth recently in the sales of organic, fair trade and natural products, and that has been driven by market forces – that's you and me selecting those products over others. Here are just a few of the issues that you can influence.

YOUR INFLUENCE ON GLOBALISATION AND CHEAP LABOUR

Some large corporations use their size, their volume of business and their ability to take their manufacturing to any part of the world where labour is cheap to undercut and undermine the marketing efforts of others. As there are many books about the dangers of globalisation, I won't dwell on this too much here. However, the practice of building factories in underprivileged and needy communities has a two-edged effect. It can be a blessing for a community to have work, but they can also be exploited. We can make sure that our Western-owned companies are aware of the need to support the communities that provide the labour in their factories, by building schools and funding community health projects. When they know we are aware and watchful they respond well. After the tsunami in Asia in 2004 it was often the large companies that were the most effective and fastest at supporting local villages and rebuilding homes and schools.

'You have the power to affect others through your choices.'

Markets need to be free and competition fair to give consumers and suppliers a fair price and to permit fair trade. Unfortunately, after many years of discussing this subject, the G8 and now the G20 (the economic councils that represent the world's wealthy nations) have yet to agree a way forward for free trade practices between nations. Exclusive trade practices stop cheap food and products coming to Europe from African countries, thus preventing them from flourishing and growing their economies. Large companies can dictate prices, which can be hard on communities that are dependent on single commodities – coffee from Brazil, Vietnam and Colombia, bananas from Ecuador, tea from Kenya and so on. But in recent years Fair Trade organisations have been set up to help consumers identify which supermarket products have been bought at a fair price from the farmers at the end of the food supply chain, and we are choosing to buy more and more of these products.

What you can do to influence globalisation

Make sure you use your power of choice. Shop around for the best options and use the internet to check up on products that give you the best value for money and the quality that you desire. Support the suppliers and farmers of developing countries by buying Fair Trade products.

Use the internet to check the background and associated companies of your favourite retailers. Often very large manufacturers subcontract, and you may find that they do not meet your own expectations regarding fair wages and conditions for employers or fair prices for farmers. Read and gain knowledge of the law and the protection that is enforceable, so that you are sure of your facts if you feel the need to protest. Boycott any product or company that does not attempt to live up to your own ethical standards.

Join a pressure group and write to the press if you find out any retailer is exploiting people anywhere in the world – not just overseas but in your own country as well. Campaign against child labour when you discover it in practice. But be aware that in rural Africa and Asia all children have to help their family finances by working in the fields – if they don't they will starve. So we need to be aware of local situations before we campaign to close factories which are the lifeblood of local communities.

Cause for hope

As I write, I have just heard on the news that a new code of conduct is in development in the UK that will ensure that the suppliers – often farmers – of large supermarkets get a fair deal, with an ombudsman to mediate disputes between the grocery trade and its suppliers.

USE PEOPLE POWER TO SAVE YOUR LOCAL SHOPS

In every country I visit there is an explosion of supermarkets, mega malls and out-of-town shopping parks. They are convenient for shoppers but they come at a price. Supermarkets, group retailers and chain stores are pushing out small traders and closing down individual high street shops. This threatens the benefits of community shopping and also the unique and distinctive shopping experiences that privately owned shops offer. It's hard for the elderly to reach the larger shops, and small community post offices and local groceries and general stores are being priced out.

'Join forces with others to use people power to save your local facilities.'

What you can do to support local shops

Make sure you support your local shops whenever you can. They will only survive if you use them. Do your best to keep butchers, post offices and other retailers in your village or high street, for once they have gone you are unlikely to get them back again.

Make use of the growing number of farmers' markets and farm shops. Buying your produce directly from source helps everyone and you get fresh produce from a local source without the added costs of transportation, wholesalers and retailers. Also, there is something rather wonderful about buying something from the person who made or grew it.

If a large supermarket is trying to get into your local town, join an action group. Recently Tesco, the supermarket chain, lost their application to build a Tesco Express in the Mill Road area of Cambridge. This was thwarted by a vigorous campaign from local residents. This is a good example of people power, the power of individuals banding together.

So we've seen that you as an individual can have influence and exert your power through the choices you make in the market-place. Let's now move on to a slightly tougher adversary – authority. Local councils, the government, the police and other institutions are often bound by bureaucracy, rules and regulations and, dare I say it, lack of imagination. They can create very interesting challenges for us as we develop our personal powers of speaking up and standing up for ourselves.

HOLDING YOUR POWER WHEN DEALING WITH AUTHORITY AND LARGE ORGANISATIONS

We all know the frustrations of dealing with a large organisation or authority, whether it be trying to get welfare payments or an appointment for a doctor, trying to change energy supplier or waiting to get through to a call centre. I myself have filed changing banks, energy suppliers or telephone companies under 'too difficult'. It can easily take me six weeks to get an appointment for my mother with her doctor because they won't release appointments more than two days ahead. This is purely caused by the necessity to maintain impressive statistics rather than satisfying the needs of their users. Let's now look at what we can do for ourselves when faced with the layers of bureaucracy that characterise many institutions. Let me share with you how I manage this. The following techniques have been gleaned via many a hard lesson!

First of all, lower your expectations. Quadruple the amount of time in which you expect to resolve your query or problem. Allow plenty of time for the conversation you are planning to have, or for the time frame of a resolution, if you need to make appointments and visit offices. This will help you keep your level of frustration within limits.

Before a phone call or appointment take three deep breaths, drop your shoulders and visualise yourself stepping into an egg with thick walls. This will put an energy barrier between you and the organisation you're about to call.

Try to be as charming as possible – throw in a few

compliments and set the scene with a positive start. This way you will get the best possible response, if there is one available. People in authority are often ready for a challenging customer or member of the public and can be disarmed by pleasantness. Remember to keep smiling at all times. If you crack and shout, you have lost the game.

When dealing with pomposity, you can use the trick suggested to me before my driving test – imagine the person naked! If this doesn't appeal, and it may well not, then know that sooner or later they will be tripped up by their own arrogance. Their karma will bring them back into line.

After a negative experience, sit down and write the most ferocious letter, expressing all your frustrations and using any language you wish. Then tear it up. When you have calmed down, write another letter making your complaint or setting out your situation clearly, without any emotion. Send that one.

These tactics are similar to those I use when travelling, as I explained in the previous chapter. I go into what I call zombie mode – emotionless, expecting anything and keeping myself calm and centred. Always avoid angry disputes, as these take your power more quickly than anything else and will leave you emotionally and physically drained.

USE YOUR POWER TO COUNTER BULLYING AND INJUSTICE

You can come across bullies anywhere, from the playground to the office and from individuals to large organisations and governments. Some instances of unjust behaviour on the part of such organisations have the feel of bullying; for example, insurance companies may not consider their delaying tactics with regard to the paying of claims to be bullying, but it smacks to me of the large and powerful organisation trying to intimidate the smaller, weaker individual.

There are many cases of large companies using their influence, their money and their lawyers to destroy the lives and the rights of ordinary men, women and children, as individuals or communities. They are often so scared of being sucked into large compensation settlements and setting a precedent for an onslaught of similar claims that they will fight tooth and nail rather than pay up. Sometimes years can go by before the victims or their families are paid, and of course in some countries they never do receive what they are due. For example, four years on there are twenty-four victims of the 7/7 London Transport terrorist attack still waiting a final compensation settlement.

Our human spirit finds injustice intolerable and it inspires our passion, our anger and our fighting spirit. Children particularly find it very difficult to deal with. As we grow up, we realise the world is not necessarily fair and we will not always be treated fairly. However, to be fully empowered we should fight injustice, bullying and unfair treatment whenever and wherever we can. Otherwise we can lose touch with our inner need to be treated fairly and equally and to see others treated likewise.

Stand up to harassment and bullying

It is important that you speak up and act for yourself whenever you can. Women in particular can face bullying, intimidation and harassment in work situations. The law in many countries now supports their rights to work and live without being sexually harassed, but there is still a way to go.

There are times when it may be necessary to stand up for yourself when you are hassled and bothered. My friends are a feisty bunch of women and several of them have had altercations where they have stood their ground – both when travelling and in the workplace. Debbie was bothered by men many times on her round-the-world gap year trip. In Egypt she reached the end of her tether, and when a man boldly put his hand up her skirt in the Cairo museum she turned around and forcibly sent him on his way. When a young man tried to grab my handbag in Johannesburg, the two girlfriends who were with me chased him down the street wielding their own bags. When Brenda was touched on the thigh by a man sitting next to her on the bus, she stood up and had to be taken off the bus for threatening behaviour with an umbrella! When I came face to face with a flasher some years ago I immediately set about chasing him (heaven knows what I planned to do if I caught him!). Paula came face to face with a man in her flat who was brandishing a knife. She looked him directly in the eye and said she felt sorry for him. She asked what was his problem, why did he feel so insecure as to be carrying a knife? After a few minutes he put down the knife and fled.

Of course, I don't condone a violent response, but it is good to have strong boundaries as to how much hassle you will take, and to take a firm stand when you are threatened by aggression or bullying behaviour.

WHAT YOU CAN DO ABOUT BULLYING

Most bullies succeed because the victim is terrified and witnesses are afraid. Be brave and report all cases of victimisation or injustice that you observe, whether they occur in the playground or in the corporate world. Same energy, different location.

Lobby, lobby, lobby your Member of Parliament on your own behalf if you are feeling unfairly treated by any authority or insurance company – in fact, any organisation, large or small. There many areas where we as citizens feel that we are not treated well, whether it be taxes, benefits, employers or banks. You have to speak up. Write to the BBC or your local television station. They will be looking for local causes to publicise.

You can take up causes for others – just *make sure you have all the facts*. It's easy to go into the fray with passion but without all the facts; you'll find yourself in the firing line, only to discover that the other party has a good case. Get the full picture if you can.

But whatever the situation, don't dismiss your power as an individual to fight causes and make changes. There are many examples where situations have been changed by the efforts of campaigners. Even individuals can turn things around using the power of the internet and the media.

Case study: The Power of You the campaigner

In 1986 John McCarthy and Jill Morrell moved into a flat together and planned their marriage. Just a few months later John had been captured in Beirut and held hostage by Shia military group Islamic Jihad. Months, then years went by without any news of John and fellow prisoner Brian Keenan. Jill decided to put her life on hold and concentrated all her efforts on working for the release of her boyfriend. She lobbied Parliament to get MPs' support and kept up a constant campaign to keep John's plight in the public eye. Five years after his kidnap, John was released. Jill has gone on to fight injustice, becoming involved in cases like that of the Bridgewater Four, four men imprisoned for eighteen years for a murder they did not commit. She is a great example of an individual who has turned around situations with her dedication, strength and courage – and with her love for John.

YOUR POWER TO STAND STRONG AGAINST CRIME

Injustice leads me to the issue of crime. I hope this will affect you only rarely, but when it does it can be disempowering and leave you feeling weak and vulnerable. If you have been the victim of a crime, it's important that you allow yourself to go through the whole recovery process that comes from the process of experience that I discussed in Chapter 2. Allow yourself to be emotional, allow the grieving, and eventually let go any attachment to the drama of the incident and forgive those involved. Otherwise the effects will last and harm you emotionally for longer than necessary. There is nothing to be ashamed of in getting counselling, if you can, to help you through this. Accept whatever assistance is offered. It may help you go through the process of forgiving if you hold in mind that most perpetrators of crime themselves come from backgrounds characterised by pain, anger and lack of love.

Mediation programmes, where perpetrators and victims of violent crime meet, have proved extremely valuable in answering the questions of 'why me?' for the victim, as well as personalising and opening compassion for the perpetrators. Although forgiveness can come slowly, if at all, those that participate in these programmes gain a greater understanding of the causes and emotions that fuel the crimes and violence. Taking part is a courageous step but it can help to give resolution for anyone who is still facing the demons of a past experience. The strength, courage and determination to move on that you show after a major incident will help those who share your life.

WHAT YOU CAN DO ABOUT YOUR SAFETY

It will make you feel stronger if you take precautions and are careful about your security. Be sensible and watch out for yourself. Check your locks and security systems. The UK police offer a service where they come and assess your home.

Don't walk alone at night or get into empty train carriages, especially if you have been drinking. Carry a pepper spray on your key ring. Never leave your drink unattended in bars and clubs where there is a chance someone may slip a sedative like Rohypnol into it. When you have to walk through dark streets or car parks, walk with confidence and stride purposefully – this will give the impression you are strong. If you look scared and vulnerable, then you are far more likely to be targeted.

'If you act strong and confident, you can persuade everyone
- including yourself'.

In South Africa, where the crime rate is high, my friends use a call-back system. They ring each other when they get home. They call it a Scotch ring – they let the phone ring three times without answering to save the cost of the call. (Sorry, Scottish friends and readers!)

Always report any form of crime, however small. The police need to know what is going on in their area and may be able to prevent problems from building up. Suffering in silence is not a good option. If your area has persistent problems with crime, then maybe consider a Neighbourhood Watch scheme.

As well as allowing you to keep an eye out for suspicious behaviour, it is also an opportunity to get to know your neighbours, and people naturally co-operate with and help those they know. Community schemes like this create a sense of social responsibility and are empowering for all involved.

IDENTITY THEFT

Identity theft is a new form of crime that has developed partly thanks to our sharing of personal information with banks, credit card companies, retail chains and internet sites. Once a criminal has your personal details they can, in your name, get credit cards, bank loans and state benefits. Posing as you, they can take money from your bank accounts and cards and get a passport or driving licence. It can be quite difficult to prove that these debts and losses are not yours, so it's sensible to be aware and on guard. This is one crime that you can avoid by sensible action.

What you can do about identity theft

Keep your pin numbers and passwords safe. Don't use telephone numbers or birth dates, as these are easy to crack. Remember also to keep your plastic cards themselves safe. I keep a photocopy of all my cards so that if I lose anything, from a driver's licence to a credit card, it's easier to cancel.

Shred all your private correspondence or old papers. It is common practice for identity thieves to delve through rubbish bins. Don't give out personal information to anyone on the phone. If the bank calls to check on your security information, tell them you will ring back and verify that the number is valid.

Remember, though, that most crimes are perpetrated by someone you know – so use your discernment. If someone in your life is getting progressively more demanding, abusive, domineering or violent, then take steps to avoid them or get help and take responsibility for your own safety.

YOUR POWER IN LIFE ROLES

....

The various roles we play in life bring different challenges and offer us different opportunities to step into our power. Let me now offer pointers and guidance on ways that you can develop and utilise the depths of your personal power in some of these roles. We will look at the roles that utilise our feminine energy of nurturer and the masculine energy of provider; remember, we all have both these energies, and they come to the fore depending on need and situation.

'You change roles several times in the play that is your life – each one is an opportunity to learn through the process of experience.'

YOUR POWER AS A PARENT

When your children are young your power as a parent is enormous, for you are their guide, instructor, teacher and carer and your influence is great. In some instances this power will be challenged and questioned by wilful, strong-minded, adventurous children. And that is how it should be, for they will only grow by testing the boundaries of their world. If you have flexible boundaries, then you will suffer until your children teach you the importance of your will, your choices and your ability to say yes or no. Nothing else in your life will teach you this so effectively. Any trip to the supermarket or playground will show you what happens when these boundaries are ineffective – you will see parents run ragged, disregarded and disempowered.

You are also the role model for your children. They will learn how to respect others by seeing the way you respect people, they will learn how to love by experiencing your own acts of love, they will learn how to respect themselves by seeing the way you respect, accept and love yourself. I get upset when a mother says, 'I am only a mother,' as this role, played out well, is the most powerful and important one on the planet. I can count on the fingers of one hand, among the traumatised and damaged people who come to me, the number who had unconditional love and support from their mother in their early years.

Unconditional love is the love you give no matter what your child has done. It is given whether they get good or bad grades, whether they are careful or careless, and it is the most accepting love of all. Unconditional love and strong boundaries, including clear messages about what is acceptable and respectful behaviour, what they can expect from the results of their actions and the basic rules of cause and effect, all assist your child to grow up to be a well-balanced and self-loving (not to be confused with self-serving) adult. The best and most powerful parenting comes from love, not from fear or guilt.

'Teach by example - you can be the blueprint for your child's understanding of love in action.'

Keeping your child safe

Your children's safety and wellbeing are obviously your greatest concern. I suggest you use the following simple prayer and meditation to visualise and send powerful, positive energies to them.

Exercise to send protective energies to your child

✧ Take a photograph of your child.

✧ Take a clear quartz crystal and hold it in your hand. Say 'I fill this crystal and programme it to hold my child . . . safe and sound.' Repeat three more times.

✧ Leave the crystal on top of the photograph in a quiet place.

✧ Now close your eyes and visualise your child smiling, happy, well and safe. Know that your child is well and safe. Say 'I call Archangel Michael to protect and keep (your child's name) safe and well. I thank all the angels for protecting and caring for (your child's name).'

YOUR POWER AS A FRIEND

You have no power of choice over your family and work team but, of course, you have the power to choose your friends and those whom you mix with socially. Through your relationships with your friends, you have the opportunity to reflect your personality and your preferences to the limit, without fear of judgement.

Friendship gives you the opportunity to flex the muscles of your power to speak up, verbalise your thoughts and express your dreams. Friends can be a sounding board for your views and allow you to clear any doubts you have about choices you are about to make. Just sharing your thoughts is a way of testing them – do they sound strong, do your arguments and logic sound convincing? Friends can provide support and advice, while friends who know you well can offer different perspectives on your plans, taking care not to take any comments as criticisms of you personally.

Case study: The Power of You to offer friendship

Debbie lost her husband suddenly last year. She lives in Australia without a family, and she says the support of her friends kept her sane in the months after his death and helped her recover her strength. Her girlfriends rang her every day and took her out for coffee, brought her little gifts to cheer her up and were available for her whenever she needed a shoulder to cry on. That's what we do for friends, we make ourselves available.

If Debbie had continued to call her friends throughout the night, taking over their lives, she would have abused the friendship and become over-demanding, which could have strained her friends' tolerance and understanding. As it was, she soon felt strong enough to cope and their relationships settled down again to a natural give and take. Everyone was empowered by the experience; they felt great because they could make a difference in someone's life. Debbie's friends developed their own compassion and ability to listen and empathise, while she felt the force of love and support just when she needed it.

If you find it difficult to make friends, or find that so-called friends are untrustworthy or fickle, then consider the amazing advantages that a close relationship without ties, expectations, emotional or legal commitments can bring. Ask yourself if you are fully open to this sort of relationship. To get the most from friendship you need to be open, responsive, and prepared to give and share all that you have and all that you are. The more you open and give, the more rewarding and empowering your friendships will become. What you learn from these trusting and close relationships will serve you well when you deal with the world at large, for they give you confidence, support, trust and experience in articulating your feelings.

YOUR POWER AS A PARTNER

Whether you marry the person you love or prefer to live together, there is a level of commitment in such a relationship that, like friendship, can offer you a great deal. A close live-in relationship offers more than company, fun and support, though these are not to be undervalued. A partnership can give you an opportunity to share yourself and to see yourself through another's eyes, allowing you to know yourself better, to find the issues that are hidden deep from strangers' eyes and to heal through expression of emotion.

It will also test you, especially if your partner is of the opposite sex. In the past the man had the say, was the head of the family and the rule maker. Now we look to be equal partners. These days women are more empowered, less prepared (thank goodness) to take a secondary or subservient role. The traditional marriage has given way to a far more equal sharing of gifts, time and roles – with house fathers and working mothers quite the norm. This means that we all have to be prepared to accept and understand each other more, to be tolerant and far more flexible than our parents and grandparents. What an ideal opportunity to show power with love, to show strength with tenderness and to speak up with compassion! We need to use diplomacy, understanding and acceptance alongside our love if our partnership is to survive.

Maybe the reason so many partnerships fail is due to this

challenge. I suggest you always see your partner as a total package – remember, no one can live up to your expectations of the perfect partner. See beyond the coping coat and focus on those aspects that work well with your energy. Oh, yes, and there are still huge differences between the way men and women see things, and between their expectations, so you will never agree or be on the same wavelength on every issue.

Let's now look at the most challenging role that you may find yourself in at any time.

YOUR POWER AS A CARER

Are you a carer? If so, you are one of the six million unpaid individuals who look after a sick, frail or disabled relative, partner or friend at home. You may find you are suffering from emotional turmoil or depression; caring for others, whether full- or part-time, can deplete your energy and spirit. It's very hard to see someone you love becoming frail, losing their memory, going blind or deaf and becoming ever more reliant on your strength, love, good will and energy. It's important, however, that you resist the temptation to put your own health needs second. Your strength, fitness and wellbeing are the support pillars both for yourself and for the person you assist.

When my mother fell last year she became totally dependent on me for her daily care. She needed help with washing, eating and all her movements. Thanks to her blood-thinning medication she suffered severe blood blisters as a result of her fall and the water tablets she was prescribed meant that every thirty minutes or so she needed a visit to the toilet. My initial reaction was to buy every gadget for the disabled known to man – several of these still sit unused at the back of the cupboard and are good for nothing but a laugh. For the first few days I was on automation and automotion, careering from one chore to the next; then my emotions started to kick in and for some time I felt absolutely dreadful. I was worried about the future, I was worried about treating her wounds, I was worried whether she was getting enough of whatever she needed – and I was worried for myself.

Yes, I must admit, I felt as though my identity, my life, had just been plucked away. How could I function as me when my entire time was taken up with caring for my mother? How could I continue to do my work, which is so time-consuming and involves so much travel? I felt as though the plug had been pulled on my life. I love my mother so much that I felt guilty even considering these issues. My heart started to thump and race and for the first time in my life I had panic attacks. I escaped into the greenhouse in the garden whenever I could, using devices such as baby monitors to keep me in touch. Gradually, though, my mother got better and we resolved that she should return to her own home with carers, which proved to be the best solution. Just as she was getting a little better my stepson became ill. I had no idea that other people's illness would have such a profound effect on my own life.

In your role as a carer it's quite natural for your emotions to swing between positive and negative. Here are some I experienced – maybe you do too:

Tired. I fell into bed exhausted every night, drained not just by the physical demands but the emotional demands as well.

Burdened by the responsibility. Here was someone entirely reliant on me. That was quite overwhelming in itself. My neck and shoulders are often tight, but at that time they morphed into concrete overnight.

Irritated. At times I felt irritated and resentful, even angry – especially as my mother, bless her heart, seemed to have lost her sharp mind. She must have had a stroke, because she had problems focusing and her memory was in tatters – especially her short-term recollection.

Frustrated. My mother lost her will and therefore couldn't be bothered with anything. My immaculate, bright mother had turned overnight into an old woman. When yet another meal was returned having hardly been touched, I fumed and cried behind the scenes. We now rely on Complan for nutrition!

Loving. Caring for my mother nevertheless brought out my compassion and the tender loving care that is usually reserved for babies and small children. Invalids do give us a chance to get in touch with our most gentle aspect.

Stronger and wiser. As I came through the initial shock of seeing my mother change so radically, and as I coped with the emotions that this brought up, I could feel myself changing too. I now can see the complete cycle of life and it has a natural beauty and sweetness about it. To see her letting go some of the inhibitions and fears that she struggled with in her life was wonderful. To see her own inner strength keep her going when her body is failing is inspiring. To be needed by her, emotionally and physically, is rewarding. I feel much stronger now. I feared what it would be like to see a loved one coming to the end of their life – now I don't have that fear any more. I have faced it and found great insights and understandings from the experience.

'The power of your love heals and supports those close to you.'

What you can do as a carer

First, make sure you get help. If you are a full-time care-giver for someone near to you, utilise whatever help you can. Many local councils and charities offer respite care breaks. If your patient demands that only you care for them, be strong and insist that you take a break. Otherwise you will become sick – and then who looks after whom? Often your patient will not be thinking as clearly as they used to, so you sometimes have to use tough love. Keep an eye on the bigger picture.

You can share your experience by reading books about people in similar situations. Sharon Snir's book *Looking for Lionel* (see appendix) describes her family's experiences looking after her mother with dementia. Or, perhaps better still, join a support group. This is especially helpful if you are caring for a disabled child – there are many groups now who give helpful advice and companionship through forums and networks.

Don't be afraid to laugh at some of the funnier episodes that occur; laughter will help raise everyone's spirits. I still smile at the time my mother took out her teeth in the middle of the evening, dropped them confidently into her whisky glass and promptly fell asleep. And don't be ashamed either. People in crisis, suffering from dementia or long-term illness or simply from the effects of old age, will change their personal habits. Take the attitude that if other people can't cope with the outcomes then that's their problem. Keep your cool.

There will be times when you will feel very guilty, days when you don't think you do enough or are patient enough, while on other days you will be bowed down with resent-ment and frustration. That is completely natural – I have been to both extremes, and sometimes on the same day.

Accept that this is just how you will be affected and find some way to release the negative feelings – not necessarily with a glass of wine or whisky, although I have found that to help! You need a confidante, a shoulder to cry on. Let out your feelings, let go and then move on.

Above all, though, don't give up hope. Great strides are now being made in the treatment of what once were incurable illnesses. Alzheimer's was once untreatable but there are medications available now, while medical researchers are learning more and more about cancer, dementia and autism. Just today I saw a report on the discovery of an underlying cause of autism. There is always room for hope, so keep checking for new breakthroughs.

Finally, remember to *go into your heart* when you have to find solutions – your heart will never lie. Use the 'Align with the power of love and step into your heart' exercise from Chapter 1.

Let us now see how power plays out in the workplace, where we live the role of provider.

YOUR POWER TO CONNECT TO YOUR STRENGTHS AT WORK

Once we step away from our families and our personal relationships of choice, we face the challenge of spending hours on end with people who come together through the circumstances of our work. Some of them will become friends and others we will find difficult and demanding, while some of the work we take on will be difficult and demanding too. You will need the attitudes and people-management skills we looked at in Chapter 3 to ensure that your work colleagues do not steal your power, while you will need to go within to ensure that you are working in the environment and job role that suits you, a role that gives you the opportunity to develop your potential and that supports and brings out the best in you.

YOUR POWER AS AN EMPLOYEE

Some people find it difficult to work for other people, as they feel the need to make their own decisions, work to their own schedule and be in control of what they do and where their work takes them. You may be one of those people, in which case self-employment can be the solution. However, you can be equally empowered working for a private company, a large institution or the government if you have the right approach. Here are some guidelines to help you hold and develop your power through your work and working environment.

First and foremost it's imperative that the work you do is right for you. The following exercise will help you find your happiness and fulfilment ratings in your current job.

Exercise to discover your fulfilment ratings

First, make a list of your strengths and skills – e.g. patience, thorough and perfectionist, great with figures, gifted writer, communicator, supportive, kind, visionary, decisive, intuitive, leader, loyal, inspirational, hard worker, athletic and fit, highly qualified. Now go through each aspect and score them between 1 and 10, based on how much your current job gives you the opportunity to use this strength/skill.

Next, mark the following statements according to how often you experience them, scoring 1 for those you experience only very rarely and 10 for those you experience all the time.

◇ You have the sense of a job well done, of satisfaction or achievement.

◇ You smile or laugh at work.

◇ You enjoy sharing your work time with your peers and colleagues.

◇ You feel appreciated and respected.

◇ Your opinions and ideas are listened to.

◇ You feel you have influence on the happiness or fulfilment of others.

◇ You feel happy to get up and go to work.

If you scored more 1–5s than 6–10s in either of the above lists, then you need to think about changing your job or career. It will be difficult to be in your personal power if you are compromising yourself daily in your choice of work. In order to be fulfilled and extended to your potential, you need to play to your strengths and skills. Even if you use work purely for a source of money and spend your free time following your dream, you will find it difficult to be fully empowered. Of course, there will be times in life when you need to compromise, but generally you should be scoring over 6 on most of the above points.

You may be struggling to find the job that does tick all the boxes for you. If so, how can you identify what will do that for you? Go back to your list of strengths, skills and qualifications. This will be the shopping list for you to find the right job. See what job your list suits most – you can get family and friends to help you with this too. If there is absolutely nothing that appeals, then see what you could learn, what extra training you could have, that would then lead you to something that suits you.

My stepdaughter Amanda worked as cabin crew with the airline Virgin Atlantic, which was the perfect job for her. She had the bubbly personality, the good figure, the sweet nature that suited her work perfectly, and she also loved to travel. Eventually, though, the long and difficult hours took their toll and she became sick and overtired. She had always enjoyed aerobics, so she decided to become a personal trainer. For this she needed the bubbly personality, the good figure and the great communication skills, but she also needed an understanding of anatomy, which she then studied. Thus she took what she had and added the necessary extra qualifications. This allowed her to move on so that she is still completely fulfilled in her work.

'You have your strengths for a reason; they are your gifts to help you do the job you came to do.'

What you can do to show your power at work

Look for opportunities to develop and use your strengths, skills and qualifications. Make sure you support your colleagues and employers, and give good value for your wages. Inspire others to be their best by role-modelling a positive attitude.

Always be in your integrity: be honest and speak and live your personal sense of truth and justice. At the same time, avoid gossip and judgement, particularly in group situations, and speak out when you come across injustice or bullying in the office, in public or the marketplace. In other words, use your influence at all levels and in all situations.

If you are ambitious, make sure you don't lose touch with

any of those points. Otherwise, on the way to the top you may step out of your own values and into the culture of your company, rather than impressing your values on the company. I know a group of women who have a sin pot in their office. If anyone, resident or visitor, is caught saying anything negative about the work, the company, themselves or someone else, they have to put a pound in the pot which is given to a local charity. You can influence the energy of your workplace – you really can.

'You have the power to influence others - use it.'

YOUR POWER IN MANAGEMENT

There are many books about management and leadership skills, so I won't presume to tread in that arena. But from the point of view of your power, there are just a few ideas I would like to share. A manager in his or her power is one who uses their strength, courage and heart to bring out the best in their staff. Here are a few pointers for gaining respect and getting the best from your staff:

✧ Admit when you are wrong.

✧ Ask for opinions and input from your staff.

✧ Never belittle or ridicule a staff member or chastise them in public.

✧ Encourage and develop the strengths and skills of your staff members and retrain them if they show weaknesses in their job role.

✧ Praise and encourage whenever possible.

✧ Be accessible. Don't see yourself as superior or above your staff.

✧ Kindness gets you more co-operation than fear.

✧ Don't be afraid to use your intuition or gut feeling – alongside experience, this can be your greatest tool.

✧ Delegate and remember the law of attachment – let go. When you let go you free yourself and allow others to blossom and grow.

✧ Use the stick with a carrot rather than to chastise.

Case study: The power of love in management

Peter was newly appointed as Production Director, so he decided to visit the most successful factory in the group and find out some of the secrets of its success – it had the least sickness absenteeism, the best production results, the least waste and so on – to use in the rest of the company. Peter started by interviewing the factory manager, Fred. He was surprised, for although Fred seemed a nice enough fellow, his under-standing of the factory process seemed ordinary if not a bit poor. He couldn't answer many of Peter's questions and said he would need to refer to his supervisors and other managers for many of the answers.

Peter was puzzled. How could Fred be running such a tight and effective operation with such poor knowledge? When he interviewed the supervisors and the workers on the shop floor, he found out. It appeared that Fred was the most understanding, kind and thoughtful manager they had ever had. Everyone loved Fred. When someone was sick, or a family member was in trouble, Fred would visit their home with flowers, fruit and gifts. When they needed help and counselling, Fred was the one to offer his spare time and

*care. When someone made a mistake, Fred was understanding
and when they needed support, Fred was there for them. So
when Fred made mistakes, or didn't understand a new process
or system, the staff did his work for him. They ran the
factory, they made sure it was up to standard. So much so
that they prided themselves on having the best-run factory
in the group!*

Always be true to who you are and see the best in
everyone who works for you. Ensure that your boundaries are strong to prevent your peers, your employer, the
public or your staff from manipulating you. Keep your
integrity and keep out of fear. And finally, ask yourself –
are you suited to management? Is this a strength of yours
or does it cause you stress? If the latter, then ask yourself
if you would be happier, more content and less fearful if
you took a role that suited your skills rather than one
that might be financially more beneficial but doesn't really
suit you.

YOUR POWER IN RETIREMENT

For some the thought of retirement is exciting, for others
it's something to dread. So much depends on how much
you are enjoying your work and whether you have provi-
sion for financial support, friendships and activities that you
can enjoy. It can be a wonderful experience, a chance to
change direction and reinvent yourself, to do the things you
have always dreamt of. Whatever you are expecting, though,
I advise you to make some plans. Otherwise it can come as
a shock, as it did for my husband, Tony.

Case study: The Power of You to change direction

When Tony retired he became quite miserable. He loved his job so much that he grieved for the loss of his work, and the camaraderie. He also felt a loss of identity. For so many years his status, his role and all that went with it had become identified with who he was. When he stepped away he had to find himself again, to ask himself – who is the real Tony Jones? He felt inadequate because he wasn't doing what he did best. Unfortunately, he felt uncomfortable in the role of DIY manager in our home, although I did push it! When I asked him to hang a picture or assemble a flat pack, he was way out of his comfort zone and this only aggravated his sense of loss. I worried that he would never find himself again, would never recognise his strengths without the need to be in the corporate world to validate himself.

However, one day he got up and made an announcement. 'I am no longer sitting around, I shall do something with the rest of my life.' Drawing up plans to do voluntary work, he came across Dormen, a local charity that offered mentoring for people running small businesses. As soon as he stepped into this new role he found himself again. He has since developed his role so that he assists new companies get started, and there is a spring in his step once more. He utilises his strengths and skills and is delighted to help. He is back on top form in his new role. He is stimulated and fulfilled; he has an identity again.

It is difficult to get paid work when you are over fifty-five years old, but there are many voluntary positions waiting for applicants. We will be looking further at opportunities to help other people and the environment in the next chapter. Whatever you do though, make sure that you find something that makes you want to get up in the morning.

Otherwise you can become completely shut down and depressed, losing your mojo as well as your power!

THE CHALLENGES OF TRANSITION FROM ROLE TO ROLE

Whenever they occur, changes in the roles you play in life present challenges. There will be times in your life when, through changes in your circumstances, you may lose touch with your vital connection with your own self – become unsure of your personal identity and your role in life. But there are ways that you can manage role change and come to find and accept a new role.

'Self-acceptance is empowering.'

LOSING YOUR SENSE OF IDENTITY THROUGH JOB LOSS OR ROLE CHANGE

Thousands of people experience loss of identity as they move from full-time work into retirement or redundancy. My father experienced something similar and he told me, 'One minute you are somebody and then the next you are nobody.' As with my husband Tony, it can hit people without hobbies particularly hard and – dare I be sexist – it affects men more than women. Women usually have more than one role right through their life – they juggle the roles of wife, mother and worker – so they are less likely to feel role-less. But loss of identity can affect a mother of young children. Going from a busy, successful career to a world of nappies, sleepless nights and baby groups is a major shift. After a few years of this it's easy for a woman to feel that her own self has been submerged as she puts family concerns before her own. Of course, there are many benefits that all mothers know about, but it doesn't stop the occasional feeling of loss and the question 'Who am I?' So it's essential that you grasp the responsibility of taking on or finding a new identity for yourself to bring yourself back into your power.

'Change is inevitable, be powerful and accept it.'

What you can do to cope with changing roles

We looked briefly in Chapter 2 at the stress that role changing can bring – here we see the impact on your self-worth. Many role changes are inevitable, while others are chosen: from school to work, from single to married, from career woman to mother, from one job to another, from worker to retiree or redundancy. If you understand the impact and are open to the change it will considerably help you to handle the experience, and it can then be an opportunity to grow and gain strength rather than a reason to suffer. And there are a number of steps you can take that will help to ease the transition.

First, if you can, prepare yourself for your new role. If you are planning retirement, start some of the activities and interests that will fill your days in the future. If you are to become a mother, read books on motherhood, attend classes, visit friends with babies, visualise yourself in your new role. Check that you really, really want to make the change. Do you have to retire? Do you really want to change jobs? If you are moving for money, ensure that your quality of life will not be compromised. Make a plan of action. This will give you some sense of control over your life and your feelings again. Give yourself something to look forward to, like a holiday with friends. Look at the power of the role you are moving into rather than the power you feel you have lost in the role that you are leaving.

If you have been made redundant (dreadful word), see it as an opportunity for a change – either a change of company or even a total career change. If you can, work part-time for a transitional period that will give you time to adapt. A staged exit will give you time to assimilate the changes and get used to your new lifestyle.

Whether your change is chosen or enforced, you may well experience a roller coaster of emotions. Allow yourself to go with the flow and understand that the emotions are a direct result of the change, and that if you allow them to flow you will come through stronger. If you try to suppress them they will hang around as unfinished business. If you have been made redundant, you may need to go through the letting go and forgiveness processes we looked at in Chapter 2. Allow yourself time to adjust to the change and to get over the grief of loss of love, status or position, independence, money or freedom – whatever you have left behind. Eventually you will start to find new activities, jobs or pastimes and then you can enjoy the benefits of your new role.

If you have time on your hands and you can't find paid work, take up voluntary work (there's more about volunteering in Chapter 6). Immediately you have an identity – you are a volunteer. This is empowering. Maybe you can help others by something you do in your home. Some of the ladies who knit for the children my charity helps are in their eighties and nineties. They are doing something useful, so they feel good. No matter what your condition, there is always something you can do. Don't let your ego stand in your way – it's better to be doing something that you enjoy or challenges you than nothing at all.

Be positive about the way you describe your role. Avoid any negative implication, such as 'I'm *only* a mother' or 'I'm doing *nothing* now, I'm retired', 'I'm *just* a secretary'. Take pride in any role you play. But don't judge yourself purely by the work you do – other people will follow your example.

Finally, keep remembering and focusing on your strengths, on those aspects of yourself that you can respect and honour. Every time you feel inadequate, bring your mind back to the positive side of your nature, your personality and your abilities.

'Look forward, when you look back over your shoulder you are more likely to trip.'

Case study: The Power of You to do the best you can

I have a healing network that is run by Apuu in Malaysia. He is a quadriplegic and confined all day to his wheelchair or to bed. For years he lived his life through others and spent most of his time reliving his previous experiences as a jockey. One day we gave him a laptop, and by placing a splint onto two fingers he learnt how to type out healing requests and send them out to the names on the register of volunteer healers. His mother told me that taking on this role changed his life; it gave him a purpose for each day. Now he keeps in touch with hundreds of people all over the world, those that ask for help and those that do the healing – he has quite a social network! He is happier and more fulfilled, and the richness of his new life shows in his face.

Many of the challenges we face affect our health. In the next chapter I will take you through some ways that you can utilise your will and inner strength to manage or combat illness and develop and control your wellbeing.

FIVE

Your Power to Heal and Be Healthy

When you are healthy you have a strong foundation on which to build a joyful life. Conversely, ill health can seriously affect your sense of personal power and destroy any sense of joy. To be truly empowered, it is important that you take responsibility for your health and wellbeing and find ways of improving it, so as to avoid slipping into chronically poor health. We become ill for a number of reasons, and in this chapter we will look at a few of them and how they can be avoided. We will also consider natural medicine and healing, which can be effective either as an alternative or a support for conventional medicine. Above all, we will share ways that you can have a sense of being the master of your own wellbeing.

'When you decide to take control of your life you are empowered.'

TAKE BACK CONTROL OF YOUR HEALTH

I believe that the state of our health is far more in our power than most of us believe. We talk about being attacked by viruses, suffering heart attacks and being victims of cancers. However, I would like you to consider the possibility that with your personal power, your strength, positive thinking, and your inner force of courage and durability, you have all you need to fend off these 'attacks'. I am convinced that we can hold up our immune system through our own positive attitude and thoughts.

Emotional upsets and discord definitely drain our energy, and when our energy levels are low we are prone to sickness. On the other hand, when we feel positive and confident through involvement in projects, work or interests, our spirits are uplifted, we feel energised and strong – able to withstand any number of bugs and viruses. Your immune system is seriously affected by low spirits and by physical, mental and emotional exhaustion and burnout. So it's important to value your health, your energy and your time, and to ensure that your boundaries are strong. When you work with claiming your power (as set out in Chapter 1) and with healing and clearing the unfinished business of your life (as in Chapter 2), when you focus on ways of training your mind to be positive about all your experiences, then you will not only be taking control of how you feel, your sense of personal power, you will also be affecting your immune system. For as your mind and spirit becomes positive, uplifted and strong, so will your body.

Before we look at specific health issues and how you can manage them, here is an exercise you can use to start each day. Use it every morning and see the difference it makes.

Exercise: Preparing your personal power for the day ahead

✧ Breathe in deeply, and as you breathe connect with the sun as it rises. Connect to the power of its energy, fill your lungs with the golden energy of strength and warmth that it radiates.

✧ Imagine your own sun in your solar plexus filling with this powerful energy. See the sun energy flowing in a golden stream, building your own sun – see your golden ball of light growing as you breathe.

✧ You are filling yourself with the force of strength. Think of yourself as a knight going into battle – put on your armour to protect yourself from any negativity you may meet today. Know your positive and strong energies will withstand anything the day can bring. All the negative thoughts and attitudes of others will just bounce off your armour.

✧ Grow tall, grow strong. Draw strength from the entire universe and all the aspects of courage it holds – the strength and courage of a lion, the solid and secure energies of mountains, the constant and unwavering force of the river flowing to the sea, moving over and around obstacles. Through your connection these are your energies now.

✧ You are strong, grounded, secure, courageous and unstoppable. So watch out world, here you come!

I recommend that, along with this meditation, you use the relaxation exercise I gave you in Chapter 2. It will calm you down at any time of day, but is particularly effective before you go to bed. Together these two exercises will help you start and end the day in control, and will help you take your wellbeing back into your own hands.

To reinforce your management of your wellbeing you need to pay daily attention to your nutrition and exercise, for these have an instant and often dramatic effect on your health and improve the functioning of your body in many ways.

'Be the master of your own wellbeing.'

NUTRITION

You need to find the right balance of food, one that suits you. Discover what upsets and irritates you, whether it be a sensitivity or an allergy, and find which foods energise you and strengthen your immune system. Be in control and take full responsibility for the everyday running of your body – try to avoid short cuts and easy options that actually deplete your energy rather than reinforce it.

Case study: The Power of You through taking control of your diet

Lorraine, a 64-year-old retired bank worker, suffered for years with bloating, overweight, heartburn, constipation, headaches and depression. 'I scratched my itchy legs until they broke out with sores. They were particularly bad when I was in the bath or bed, so obviously heat was not good. I went from one skin specialist to another and they were not able to diagnose what was wrong with me.

'On 27 July 2007 I went to a homeopath and iridologist. He took one look at me and told me I was gluten intolerant. He assessed me and gave me the list of food that

I should and should not eat. I gave away four bags of food with gluten in it. I changed my way of eating a week later and by November 2007 had lost 14 kilograms of weight, I went from a size 38 to 36 with no exercise. I weighed 72 kilograms and am now 58 kilograms.

'*I started off on salads with chicken or fish but soon got fed up with that. Then I introduced rice or potatoes with vegetables and chicken. I take a multivitamin every day, along with 1,000 milligrams of vitamin C, lecithin and a viral tablet to boost my immune system.*

'*I am less stressed and angry, I am sleeping less yet I have more energy. And no more headaches, which I had every day. I feel alive and motivated again.*'

EXERCISE

Regular exercise can definitely start an upward energetic spiral of your spirits, your mind and your body. Thanks to our holistic nature, as we revitalise our body by strengthening our bodily muscles, developing our heart muscle and clearing our arteries, we also strengthen our mind and spirit and clear out toxic thoughts and emotions.

Choose the exercise routines that suit you best. Running, jogging, swimming and rowing are all examples of aerobic exercise that stimulate heart activity and enhance metabolism, and which don't depend on other people. Weight work in the gym and other power activities build muscle. Competitive team sports have the advantage of offering social connections too. Walking, though, is still my favourite, as it gives me a chance to contemplate and enjoy closeness with nature. Set up an action plan for your exercise and make it part of your empowerment objectives.

TAKING THE FEAR FROM VIRUSES

'Positive attitudes strengthen your immune system.'

Positive thoughts and attitudes help strengthen the natural immunity that enables you to ward off viruses. They also help to combat the fear that can run through society when the media get hold of stories about a pandemic. It's possible to hold strong against many infections, resisting them through determination and will power. You may have noticed that if you have been particularly busy, you may get sick once your holiday starts – when your guard is dropped and you relax. Recently my husband and my friend's husband were both laid low with the norovirus that causes vomiting and diarrhoea; I caught it only very mildly, and my friend didn't get it at all. Whereas the men are retired, we both felt we were too busy to get sick.

WHAT YOU CAN DO TO AVOID VIRUSES

There are several things you can do to improve your chances of avoiding viruses. Of course, you should always take sensible precautions not to be exposed. But make sure you also maintain a positive approach. Keep your language positive and when your mind plays tricks and fearful thoughts start to rise, say something positive to counteract them. If your mind is saying 'I think I feel ill', say 'I feel absolutely fine, never fitter'.

Avoid exposure to the fear. Avoid reading, rereading and listening to every news bulletin on approaching pandemics. Don't spend hours hyping up what you have heard with friends and family, unless you can bring a positive slant.

Care for your natural immune system by ensuring you follow good lifestyle practices, such as a well-balanced diet with plenty of vegetables and fruit, plenty of water, plenty of sleep, and plenty of exercise. The intention of caring and respecting your body will lift you spiritually and help strengthen your holistic defence system.

Lift your spirits by doing those things that uplift you: music, dance, walks in the country, helping others – whatever floats your happiness boat. The happier you are, the less likely you are to succumb. And if you do catch a virus, don't fight it by continuing to work too hard. Rest your body and mind and use the time to contemplate, read and relax. You may have caught it just so that your mind and body can chill and take time out.

Case study: Bobo – The Power of You through determination

Dr Cary Rasof, my partner in Hearts and Hands for Africa, our charity in Zambia, found Bobo lying sick and dying in a nearby village. He had Stage Four AIDS and TB. His wife had left him and he was staying in his brother's hut, where his main sustenance was alcohol. His spirit and hope had deserted him. So Cary started to bring him good nutritious food, the high protein diet that was good for his condition, and ensured that he took his medicine. After a while Bobo started to get stronger, helped by the nutrition, the medicine and the sense of being valued enough to receive support from a stranger. Cary discovered that he had been a teacher and encouraged him to start classes for the village orphans. He took this opportunity, gave up drinking, took a small loan to start a business buying and selling oil and held daily classes outside his house.

When he decided to 'come out' about his health problems, the local families unfortunately withdrew the children due to a strong stigma against AIDS sufferers. However, after a brief relapse he recovered his positive nature and continued to grow from strength to strength, and he is now a full-time teacher at a school. When I visited this year he asked if he could have help setting up a support group for other people with HIV and AIDS in his community. Well done, Bobo – he is now a role model and inspiration, thanks to his personal determination reinforced by help from a stranger.

You can find out more information about the work of Hearts and Hands for Africa on www.heartshands.org.

Before I leave the subject of viruses, I should mention that significant danger comes from strains of disease that cross over from animals and birds to humans. From a spiritual standpoint, I believe that we increase the risk of the animal kingdom negatively affecting us through karmic retribution as we continue to mistreat animals, hunt them to extinction and destroy their habitat. When we start to fully respect the world of nature, the chances of humans suffering from such animal-borne diseases will be greatly reduced.

COPING WITH SERIOUS DISEASE

All sickness can make you feel out of control of your life, and we will be looking in a moment at the spiritual and emotional effects of illness and what you can do to alleviate these. I don't intend to take you through the full range of illnesses and disabilities, but I would like to touch on a couple of aspects of illness that I have experienced that can be real threats to our energy and will demand your strength and determination to resist them.

It can be devastating to learn that you have contracted a serious illness, and naturally we all feel very frightened when we get the news. However, it's important to know that every illness has survivors and that, given good treatment and strong support, your own natural will to overcome the illness can take you a long way towards recovery. I have mentioned before our holistic make-up, the link between our mind, our emotions and our body – this is the key. Your most powerful medicine is hope, strength, courage and the determination to come through, alongside the love you have for life and the respect you have for your body and yourself. Through the deployment of these qualities, coupled with support from friends, family and the medical profession, your illness can be a journey of triumph. For most of us, facing the challenge of illness is the most powerful of our life's experiences. It draws on all our resources and takes us deep within. I have seen many friends and clients find true inner peace as they make this deep connection while going through the greatest challenge of their lives.

If you contract a serious disease it's important that you give yourself the space, the time and the energy to take on the challenge. This is a time to be self-centred and self-focused as you give yourself the attention you need – attention that you may not have been giving yourself in the past. From my own personal experience, and that of friends and clients, I have drawn a number of points that you may like to bear in mind, and that may help you on this stage of your life's journey.

What to do if diagnosed with a serious illness

When you get the news, allow yourself to go through the natural emotional roller coaster that will come from the shock of hearing about your illness and the implications that it brings. Cry freely. If you feel angry, be angry – be mad with yourself, God, the world and so on without restraint. Don't bottle up your emotions at this stage – taking the stiff upper lip approach will not serve you. If you suppress your feelings, they can fester inside you and make you feel worse. If you want to spare your family, find a friend or counsellor to unburden your feelings.

Have a look at the staggering success rates that are now achieved by modern medicine. Just as an example, testicular cancer now has a 95 per cent recovery rate. Read uplifting survivor stories such as those in *Chicken Soup for the Soul* by Jack Canfield.

Take whatever complementary medicine and therapy feels right to supplement your treatment, assist with pain control and counter the toxic effects of radiotherapy and chemo. Acupuncture, massage, Reiki and spiritual healing can all help you feel better and relieve some symptoms. Be strong-minded and choose to do whatever feels good for you. Integrated medicine – a mix of conventional and complementary – can be a powerful way forward.

Make sure you accept counselling, support and love from friends. They will want to help, so don't be shy to ask for their help. Let them cut your grass on your off days or do your shopping.

Visualise yourself well and recovered and try not to go down too many negative paths. Keep a goal of recovery, but don't do it just for the sake of others, as this can mean you suppress your fears.

There could be a reason why you became ill. When recovering, you can work through understanding this. Maybe you put too much of yourself into your work. Maybe you really don't enjoy your work. Maybe your lifestyle was unhealthy. Maybe your mindset was negative. Maybe you still hold old bitterness and anger from past experiences. Take your time and eventually have a deep look at yourself from inside out. If you feel like it, get help with your healing process.

'Use an illness as a cue for a life change and a new way to appreciate yourself.'

When you are sick, you feel particularly vulnerable and may feel all your power has left you. However, there is a source of strength and support that is always there for you. Whether healthy or sick, you need to take time to connect to a source of spirit support.

YOUR SPIRITUAL CONNECTION – A GREAT SOURCE OF STRENGTH AND SUPPORT

Whenever you face challenges in life, your greatest strength can come from beyond the material realm – it can come from your personal spiritual connection to universal spirit. You can connect directly to your sense of spiritual divinity through meditation. This is the act of going within and connecting through your senses and mind. Here are a few points to bear in mind when meditating in this way, followed by an exercise of a guided visualisation to help you make your own divine connection.

GROUNDING

Always ground yourself before you start. This prevents your consciousness from leaving your body, creating a sense of otherworldliness and detaching you from reality. Here are two ways you can help to ground yourself:

✧ Visualise yourself as a tree with roots growing down into the Earth beneath you. See the roots growing deeper and deeper, connecting you energetically to Mother Earth.

✦ Visualise yourself sitting on a beach and feel your toes digging deep into the sand.

You can use crystals and essential oils to help you to become grounded and energetically stabilised before and while you meditate. Obsidian, Tourmaline and Red Agate are all crystals that are good for grounding. Hold them in your hands while you meditate. Or you can use essential oils created from plant extracts. Particularly powerful are tree essences: Spruce, Pine, Vetivert and Fir.

PROTECTION

Always protect your energy field before you meditate. I have covered protection in depth in my book *Healing Negative Energies* and also in Chapter 3 of this book. Protection prevents you from being affected by any negative or intrusive spiritual influences. As I have already described, one means of protecting yourself is to visualise a violet flame surrounding you. This clears your energy and protects you.

DISTRACTIONS

You may be distracted by background noises and thoughts that push their way in when you are meditating. Don't worry about them, invite them in and continue. If you try to push them out they have a habit of getting quite forceful and become even more intrusive! Don't worry if you doze off or fly away somewhere else, just bring your focus back when it feels right. There are no right and wrong ways to do this

– just accept whatever you see and experience as being what you need and right for you.

Meditation for unity with spirit

It will help you to make your own connection to your spiritual master, God, divine presence or nature – whatever fulfils your personal spiritual need. If you have an established faith, connect to the deity of your choice.

Take plenty of time for this meditation and use it whenever you feel disturbed, off centre and out of harmony with yourself or others, stressed, unhappy or alone and unloved. It will allow you to extend beyond your own physical body, thoughts and emotions to a greater and more expansive expression of yourself.

✧ Find a quiet place where you can relax uninterrupted for some time. Turn off phones and televisions and create a space that is sacred to you. This may be outdoors in a garden, or it may be in a room with something that brings you to a peaceful state of mind and draws your focus – for example, a candle, an incense burner, a crystal, a Bible, or a picture of a divine presence, a spiritual leader or a beautiful scene.

✧ Place your feet flat on the ground or adopt the yoga lotus position, with your legs crossed and knees up close to your body. If you lie flat you may be tempted into sleep!

✧ Protect yourself by visualising or sensing a violet flame burning around you, clearing away all negative energies and placing you in a shield of protection.

✧ Close your eyes and drop your shoulders.

✧ Visualise yourself as a great tree. See your roots growing down into the Earth beneath you, through the Earth's surface, going down, down, deeper and deeper. You are stabilised now, you are secure, you are grounded and at one with the loving, supportive energies of Mother Earth. Take a moment or two to enjoy the peace of being still and in the present.

✧ Take four deep breaths through to your stomach. Let your body get softer and more and more relaxed.

✧ You are at peace, all is well. All your attention is focused on yourself and your intention to connect to your sense of the purity of spirit.

✧ A pure white light is pouring over you now; it envelops you and caresses you. It is unconditional love. It enters your physicality – it flows through to every particle of your being. Sense and know that this love is connecting and binding with the love that is the true core of your being.

✧ Visualise a great flame within you, growing stronger and stronger as the love that is your essence of being and the love that flows through the entire universe in every part of creation come together in great union.

✧ You are totally connected now to the spirit that is within everything in the world, in every living being, in every stone, stick, crystal, every mountain and rock, in every stream, river and ocean, every cloud, every rainbow, every sunset, in every animal, every bird, every plant, every tree. You are united as one with this perfect stream of spiritual energy. You are united by the power of love. Feel the strength and the power that this unified love gives you.

> ✧ Take time to feel yourself expand beyond your personal
> spiritual and physical limitations to be complete with all
> that is.

When you have completed this exercise, take some time
to relax before you drive or use machinery, for you have
experienced an extension of your consciousness and aware-
ness beyond your own body that may leave you feeling a
little spacey. In time you will come back to Earth.

TAKING BACK CONTROL FROM ADDICTIONS

Dependency on any addictive substance or behaviour is
naturally disempowering. Addictive products draw our energy
out and beyond through yearning and craving; they hold us
in their control so that we let go our ability to manage our
desires and they encourage us to give in to an external force.
Addiction can bring sickness, as in the case of tobacco, drugs
and alcohol, and the dependence and actual thrall of addiction can destroy us emotionally, spiritually and physically. In
other words, they don't do us any good! Guess what – we
all know this, yet we continue to spend our money on these
substances that harm us. Let's look at some of the statistics
readily available on the net:

✧ Smoking-related diseases kill one in ten adults, causing
four million deaths a year.

✧ In the USA, alcohol and drug abuse are implicated in
three-quarters of all domestic abuse, rapes, child molesta-
tions, suicides and murders.

✧ In the UK in 2008–9, 10 per cent of adults and 22 per cent of young adults had used one or more illicit drug.

✧ In the UK in the same period, 42,000 hospital admissions were related to drug use.

CIGARETTES

In the last few years we have all been made aware of health risks as the government and tobacco companies issue warnings. If you smoke nowadays, you know that smoking isn't good for your health and you can end up with lung or heart problems.

What you can do about smoking

The best action you can take if you are a smoker is to stop! I based my own withdrawal on information sent to me by ASH (Action on Smoking and Health – see appendix for details). First, choose a time when you have little stress and few social dates. Avoid the places where you smoke the most and the food or drink that you associate with smoking, and ask your friends to support you. Keep in mind that you are taking control of this addiction – see it as part of your journey to empowerment. Choose a goal date for freedom day and each day drop off one cigarette.

Set up a visualisation involving something that would revolt you. I absolutely detest porridge, so my visualisation was of a bowl of porridge with a cigarette stuck into it and being told to eat the lot. Urgh! Every time you have a craving, bring on the visualisation.

Here are some thoughts to ponder on: you are not *giving anything up*. You are *gaining* better health – your lungs and heart will immediately start to improve, your breath will smell sweeter. You are gaining financially – think what you will do with the money, maybe a holiday or a gift to yourself. You are gaining an improved sense of taste – food will start tasting better. And finally, most important of all, you are gaining *empowerment* – you are now back in control.

ALCOHOL

Drinking can limit your personal power as control is transferred from you to alcohol; once an outside force has control over you, then you are disempowered. This can be true even if you are not addicted. More than a third of British adults drink more than the safe daily alcohol limit of three to four units a day. We do need to keep a balance between becoming paranoid about the effects and demonising a social pint – however, there is no doubt that excessive drinking is bad for health. So moderation is the key. If you do over-indulge occasionally, however, try not to judge yourself too harshly, for the guilt will probably do you more harm than the alcohol.

What you can do about your drinking

If you feel that drinking is a habit that is in control of you, whether it be at a social level or you have become alcoholic, then take the matter into your own hands and seek help. You can start with your GP who can give you literature, guidance and, if necessary, medication. The very act of going for help is an empowering action. AA (Alcoholics Anonymous – www.aa.org) offers tremendous support and guidance not only to heavy drinkers, but also to their families.

'The present moment is the most powerful place to be.'

There are two key concepts to the success of Alcoholics Anonymous and other support groups. The first is living in the moment – taking one step at a time and not worrying about what you are going to do tomorrow. By not drinking today, you avoid getting drunk today. The second is the offering of support not judgement – countering the feelings of guilt, loneliness and helplessness that the illness of alcoholism brings with it.

If you are trying to stop drinking, the following exercise may help you to focus on taking action not to drink today.

Exercise to be in control of the moment

✧ Close your eyes and reflect on your problem. Is it your wish to feel stronger, more in control of your life?

✧ See yourself sitting in the middle of the universe. The world is at your feet and the planets and stars are around you. The spiritual law of the universe is that whatever you want, need, and desire can be manifested – the entire energy of the universe is focused on responding to your intention.

✧ Do you confirm that your intention is to be healthy and strong, untouched by the outside forces of alcohol? If so, say so out loud three times.

✧ Know that the rest of your life is divided into a series of time slots and that the only one you need to consider is the one you are in at this moment – today. Each day is split into minutes – you are only concerned with this minute. You need only to concern yourself that in this minute you are in control and the drink is not.

✧ Whenever and if ever you feel the pull towards drink – maybe when you feel stressed or confused – remember, 'Not in this minute'.

DRUGS

Over time, hard drugs have extreme effects on health and peace of mind. Although their initial effect can be uplifting and inspiring, the ongoing use of drugs and the cost of addiction can and frequently does destroy life. I believe most users are looking for the empowerment and happiness that is the focus of this book. They sense that there is an aspect of life, of spirit and inner wellbeing that they may be finding elusive.

'The desire to heal, to change your life, to get stronger is the first step of healing and empowerment - do you have that desire?'

What you can do about drug-taking

Do you think you can step around the shame that you feel? Do you think you can accept that you have a problem? Do you think you can ask for help?

If you can answer honestly 'yes' to any of these questions, or better still all of them, you are definitely on the right track to recovery! Your desire to take back your life from the influences of an outside force is taking back self-responsibility, the first step to taking back your power. There are many organisations, charities and support groups run by volunteers, health experts and people who have been through exactly the same situations you are in − your next step is to find the one that suits you. Please see the appendix for details.

Case study: The Power of You to help others with your experiences

In Keighley, Yorkshire, there is a group of former addicts who are now helping others by sharing their own experiences of drug and alcohol addiction. The group is called Choices. They share their stories and give support to those who are still struggling with addiction. One of the volunteers told her story: she had always been a heavy drinker, drinking a bottle of wine a night, but could always function – until her drinking got out of hand. At that point things got so bad that she couldn't work and her family were severely affected. Although she admitted that she used drink to help her with her problems, eventually she recognised that her main problem was the drink itself. She tried to take her life and was hospitalised, at which point she decided to take the situation in hand. She sought help and with support she gave up drinking. Since then she has been helping others do the same and take back control of their lives.

'It is more empowering to ask for help rather than to suffer alone.'

All addictive practices – smoking, drinking, drug-taking, gambling, sex, internet and phone messaging, electronic games and so on – mask underlying causes. Do you have any addictive habits? If so, let's take a look to see why and consider what you can do to deal with these.

WHY DO WE DO IT?

All addictive practices and substances give an instant high: the gambler's winning lift, the buzz of drugs, the calming effect of nicotine or the uplifting rush of alcohol. You may have an underlying need that causes you to use tobacco, alcohol or drugs; they are used to mask your inner pain. The way to empowerment is through healing the causes of this pain – the childhood scars, the unfair and hurtful experiences, the rejection and betrayals and the loss of loved ones.

What you can do about addiction

If you heal the causes, you won't need these costly and harmful products. In my books *Heal Yourself, Opening Your Heart* and *The Soul Connection* I share many ways that you can work through the healing process of betrayal, abandonment, guilt, rejection, grief which cause confusion, loss of faith, distrust of self and others, lack of confidence, helplessness, panic attacks, loneliness, low self-esteem and so on. Rather than judge someone for taking drugs or drinking to excess, we need to look behind the scenes, dig deeper, to discover what emotional disturbance is driving the person to find a 'cure' or 'fix'. There are many books on ways to help clear your addictions, such as Patrick Holford's *How to Quit without Feeling S**t* (see appendix for details).

'Remember, whatever your perceived weaknesses are, they just mask your inner strength and power - never forget it is there waiting to be claimed.'

A happiness quest

Many of my clients tell me they started their own personal quest of healing, finding a way out of the murk of their emotional pain, when they hit their deepest and darkest moment. This might have been triggered by the realisation that a substance was in control of their lives, or by a broken marriage, a job loss or a major illness. It's never too late to start the journey of recovery. Before you can do this, though, you need to know yourself, and you will need honesty and courage to dig deep within. If you are a sufferer from any form of addiction, the next exercise can help you find out why.

Exercise: Why?

✧ Find a quiet space without interference from phones or family. Take your journal and think back into your past, think about your feelings, what masks you wear. Make a list of the most disturbing events of your life. Ask yourself how these affected you at the time. What did you feel, what did you do as a result?

✧ Ask yourself how you feel about them now. Do they still trouble you? Do you suffer anguish, self-doubt, distrust, hate, panic, etc. when you connect with the situation or the outcomes? What do you intend to do about healing these feelings?

✧ Ask yourself, did any of these situations cause you to change your behaviour, attitude or perception of yourself or people in general? What would it take to bring back the trust, love and acceptance that is your true state?

✧ Think about what course of action you can take to bring yourself back to that state.

Action of any sort will give you a sense of taking control and will help get rid of the lethargy, hopelessness and help-lessness that pervades these problems. On the next page are some suggestions to start your healing journey.

'Action is your power tool.'

Books. Read about your particular problem – the symptoms, the emotional causes and the root cause.

Support. Join support groups such as Alcoholics Anonymous.

Help. Seek medical help.

Alternative therapies. Visit therapists – anything from acupuncture to reflexology can start to unwind the emotions and stress that push us to hide symptoms.

Dig deep. Set the intention to heal yourself and go deep within to find your own root cause, or the causes of the symptoms that drive you to addiction or excess.

Exercise. Take up yoga, Tai Chi or another spiritually driven exercise routine.

Interests. Take a course or holiday based on an interest, such as painting, cooking, woodcraft, etc. This will give you something positive to focus on.

Retreats. Spiritual or healing retreats are particularly helpful and can help you fast-track your healing process. I run retreats in the UK and overseas every year and the results have been profound. They give you a chance to focus on yourself exclusively and allow you to go deep within without interruption and distraction from your daily life. Details are on my website (see appendix).

Counselling. Find counselling for your particular problem.

Releasing remorse. Negative habits, addictions and compulsive behaviour are almost always accompanied by feelings of remorse and guilt. You may benefit from working through the exercises in Chapter 2 to help release these feelings.

Positive focus. List all the benefits of life where the control comes back to you, for example finance, health, social life, inner feelings, etc. Focus on the positive state that you will be in without your addiction.

Choose the route that you feel best suits your situation and that draws you most strongly. Write down the direction you have chosen in your journal and each day allocate some quiet time to spend holding this intention firmly in your mind. Saying your intention out loud will help to anchor and focus on positive outcomes.

HEALTH CARE – YOUR CHOICE

We'll now consider the choices you have when you seek a solution for a physical problem. First we will look at the challenges you may face in the traditional medical system. We will then look at other options – alternative and complementary health care systems and your own power of healing.

In the UK we are extremely fortunate to have an established health service, giving support and health care to everyone no matter what their means. As with all national institutions, there are plenty of opportunities to deride or criticise it, but it's a true blessing that perhaps only becomes apparent and fully appreciated when we travel to places where it does not exist. Any institution that has such a broad scope of responsibility will come under pressure at times, so it may not always meet our expectations. However, there are many ways that you can retain your power, in order to progress your treatment and be personally involved in your recovery process. Whenever and wherever you have the opportunity to make personal choices, please do so and use your free will. These days it is perfectly acceptable to question your doctor, to ask, for example, exactly what your prescription will do and if there are any side effects.

CHOICES OVER VACCINATIONS

There are many diseases that affected and killed our ancestors that are just not part of our lives any more, thanks to vaccinations. The health organisations in the USA and Australia are totally committed to these benefits and MMR vaccinations, for example, are compulsory by law. Currently we can choose whether or not to vaccinate against MMR in the UK – although there are moves to change this. If you are affected by the discussions in the media on the possibility of autism from these vaccinations, you may be faced with a difficult decision when your children are due for their MMR vaccinations.   I would suggest you keep in mind the value of vaccinations generally to prevent so many illnesses. If you feel strongly that we should continue to have a choice, then join one of the campaigns – just Google 'compulsory vaccination UK' to find them. There are, however, different viewpoints about the value of vaccinations; maybe Debbie's situation may help you when faced with this difficult decision.

Case study: The Power of You to make informed decisions

Debbie had a decision to face when her baby was due for MMR vaccination while she lived in Hong Kong. She was wary of giving such a tiny child so many inoculations in one go and concerned about their effects. The many reports around at that time about the dangers of inoculation made it hard for her to come to a decision. She decided to seek advice from someone she trusted who had professional experience, so she rang her mother-in-law, a practising GP in Scotland. As a doctor her mother-in-law's advice was clear: she had seen children suffering from the horrendous consequences of measles, mumps and rubella and wouldn't hesitate for a moment to recommend that Debbie accept the vaccines for her child.

Debbie took her advice and immediately stepped out of the stress of doubt and uncertainty. She has never regretted her choice – as she said, 'There was so much conflicting advice I didn't know which way to turn, but after speaking to my mother-in-law, who I could trust, I could see that I just didn't want to take a chance. It was amazing how strong I felt once I made up my mind.'

Doing something from fear or because you feel you are bullied into it will make you feel disempowered. However, when you exercise your power of choice you are empowered. I suggest that you read all the available advice and make your own mind up whether you want vaccinations for yourself or your family.

'Knowledge and understanding feed your personal power – gather the facts and then make your decision.'

CHOICES OVER MAMMOGRAMS AND SCREENING

Similarly, the debate over the pros and cons of mammograms for breast cancer screening goes on. This process involves taking an X-ray during which the breast is pressed between two metal plates. It's painful and controversial. Whether you have a mammogram or not, it's a good idea to do your own detective work, checking your breasts regularly. Your doctor will show you how, or you can find information on the internet. Make regular trips to a gynaecologist and take advantage of any health checks that are on offer, such as the bowel cancer screening that is now available free in the UK for the over-sixties.

CHOICES OVER DRUGS

When you are to be prescribed drugs, take an interest in the selection and use the vast amount of information available to help you be more informed about the drugs chosen. In fact, always discuss your options with your doctor when he gives you any pills or potions. Drug companies do pressurise doctors to promote their brands, while for obvious reasons the health service tries to use cheaper options when it can. Read the leaflet that comes with the medicine and take responsibility for your entire treatment process. If you suffer any side effects at all from your medication, don't grin and bear it but report back to your health care provider.

There are several other things to remember. Don't buy medicine from the internet unless it is from an accredited supplier. There are many unscrupulous sites who sell copy brand names – not generic medicine, but fake drugs that are totally useless, packaged in copy boxes posing as the real thing. Some are contaminated, while others contain nothing more than starch and talcum powder.

If you are suffering from a condition that needs long-term medication, you may like to consider what alternative or complementary medicines and therapies are available that may help improve your condition. I will look further into these at the end of this chapter.

'By looking at all your options you are taking self-responsibility. Self-responsibility is the foundation of your personal power.'

HOSPITAL

If your illness or suspected illness takes you to hospital, make sure you are mentally prepared. It can be an overwhelming experience to put yourself totally in the hands of medical staff, and you may have a sense of being vulnerable. So make sure you are as fully informed as possible Before you go into hospital: find out as much as you can about your condition, any treatment or any possible operation you might need. You have more chance of being treated with respect if you are an informed and knowledgeable patient.

While in hospital, be proactive when you can. If you feel that you have been forgotten by the nursing staff, gently remind them you are still there. If you know you are supposed to have a particular medication, make sure they bring it. Take as much responsibility as you can within the limitations in which you find yourself.

If you are very ill, you may have to face decisions and difficult situations while in hospital. It will help you tremendously if you have a champion – someone to support you who will speak up for you and discuss your situation with surgeons and doctors. You need all your energy for recovery. Let someone else act on your behalf!

Protect yourself from negative energies. When you are in hospital you may be affected by the energies of other patients, so employ a protective energy like the violet flame while you are there. I use protection spray to help me, whether I am a patient or just visiting. Debbie, who creates essential oil blends at Ripple, gave her friend who recently went into hospital a bottle of Patience and a bottle of Nurture – Patience to combat the frustration and Nurture for the weepy times. She used up both bottles!

Finally, visualise yourself well. Our minds have a strong power over our bodies, as we have already discussed. Think yourself well and recovered; visualise yourself fit and well. See yourself busy with your life, without the problem that brought you into hospital. Although your body may be feeling under par, you can use your spirit to bring you through this difficult time. Remember, your mind, spirit and body work together. The next exercise will help strengthen your power of self-healing.

Exercise: The Power of You to heal

Following this exercise is one of ways that you can use alternatives to medication supplied by the pharmaceutical companies and processes other than those of conventional surgery. I personally think there is a good argument for using both, and for letting your common sense and your intuition guide you to the method that suits you best in any given situation.

✧ Acknowledge your spirit as the inner strength that can bring you through any challenge if it's your will to do so. Close your eyes, drop your shoulders and relax your body.

✧ If you have any spiritual beliefs, access your masters and angels through prayer and ask for help to keep your spirit strong.

✧ As you breathe, access your core energy of your personal power. Sense it in your solar plexus, below your ribs, and see it as a golden light that gets stronger and stronger on each breath. See it radiating through your entire body, filling every part. Take it to those parts that are hurting to give strength.

✧ See the golden light fill the pain. Ask your body to let the pain dissolve into the light.

◆ Now focus on your heart centre in the middle of your chest and see love radiating from here. See this love radiating through your body. Think of your body with love and respect. Send the love to the parts of you that are hurting and see the love filling every muscle, joint and organ. Relax into the healing energy of love.

◆ Know that this powerful fusion of strength and love has the ability to uplift your spirits and heal your body.

ALTERNATIVE WAYS TO EMPOWER HEALTH AND WELLBEING

In recent years there has been a growing interest in alternative healing methods such as vitamins, supplements, herbal medicines and natural energy healing such as Reiki. As we take more responsibility for our own health, many of us are looking for remedies that have more natural ingredients and less chemical substance. I sense that scientists, medical practitioners and alternative and complementary therapists will grow closer and closer in the future, and offer integrated health solutions that will solve most of our health issues.

'Nature has all our answers.'

At present we may feel our choice over conventional medication is limited; however, we do have the power of choice when we use therapies and alternative or complementary supplements and remedies. As a spiritual healer, I work in the area of natural and alternative therapies and medicine, and I have seen some extremely successful outcomes from their use. Let me begin by sharing the power of spiritual healing.

SPIRITUAL HEALING

I have been a healer for some fifteen years and I love it. It can be extremely effective without being intrusive and doesn't create painful physical side effects. It is an empowering process because it is a joint venture – the client and I create an energy bond and jointly hold the intention for change. We use the high frequency energy of love to transform the sickness, the disharmony and the emotional pain. Healing can touch aspects of you that have been in trouble since childhood. It can clear genetic attitudes and feelings that have been passed through generations, release grief that has been deeply hidden, clear the burden of guilt and dissolve the bitterness and anger that disturbs or even prevents close and loving relationships. It is a beautiful and natural process. Here is a brief overview of the process I use:

Connection of energy at soul, heart and Higher Self (the latter is the spiritual aspect of an individual that holds the wisdom of their past experience from their current and previous lifetimes). This can operate over the phone or through the internet, for individuals or for groups.

Intention. My client holds their intention to heal. I set my intention to assist the healing with love; to act as a conduit for the universal energies of love and compassion.

Love. I then guide my client to open their heart, enabling them to receive the love they need in order to lift their energies to a level where a transformation can occur, returning harmony to all aspects of their being – mind, body and spirit. The energies of love move to wherever they are needed.

Outcomes. These vary, but all clients feel a sense of relaxation and a sense that heavy energies such as stress, fear, guilt and worry have lifted. Through the holistic connection the body too can heal.

You too can access your personal power of healing. With the following simple process you can assist in the clearing of negative energies and help to lift the overall energy of another person (or yourself) through the input of high vibration energy – the energy of universal, unconditional love. Just follow these simple steps and offer your own love and care to the person receiving.

Exercise: The Power of You to heal naturally

✧ Place a bowl of water containing sea salt close to where you and the recipient of your healing will be sitting.

✧ Protect yourself by visualising the violet flame, or use protection spray (see Chapter 3 on protection methods).

✧ Visualise yourself surrounded by a ball of pink light of love.

✧ Visualise yourself and your recipient surrounded by a circle of blue light that only love can enter. You have now created a beautiful space in which to give your healing.

✧ Sweep your hands through your recipient's aura and know that you are clearing away all the blocks and thought forms of stress and worry that have accumulated from negative and stressful thoughts, or have been picked up from other people who they have met.

✧ Flick the negative energies from your hands into the bowl of salt. (Throw this into a drain when you have finished.) You can imagine this energy being transformed back to light.

✧ Then use the symbol shown below to invoke the universal energies of love and compassion. Draw it three times in the air, which will open you to receive the healing energies. This means you channel the energy rather than deplete your own energy force.

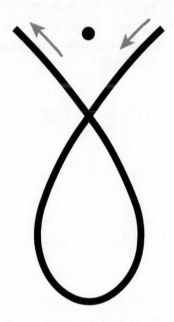

✧ Place your hands on or over the recipient, wherever you feel they need the healing energy. If they need an all-over boost, then place your hand or hands over the crown chakra on the top of their head. If they have a specific problem, focus the energy on that. Continue for as long as you feel or sense the energy is flowing. You may feel a slight pulsing in your hands as the energies flow. The recipient may feel tingling sensations as you clear and lift their energies.

✧ Seal the healing with a hug!

Remember, you can do this on yourself as well. Just direct your hands and the healing energies to your own trouble spots. You can do no harm at all with this loving process, but do avoid sweeping upwards on a person's body, as you will be sweeping negative energies towards their head. And don't put your healing hands on a physical heart with a pacemaker, as this can disturb its rhythm.

There are many other non-intrusive therapies that work on the entire body system. They can be extremely supportive to the conventional medical treatment you may be receiving, for they work on healing and balancing your mind, emotions and spirit, and support your body in its recovery process. Here are a few I have tried:

Reflexology. This is a form of therapy used by the Chinese for centuries. The therapist presses on points of the foot that are linked to every part of the body by energy lines known as meridians. As the pressure is put on the foot, the energy clears blocks along these lines and allows the vital life force energy to flow again, revitalising the joints, organs and muscles. It works well for clearing lymph glands and for reducing water retention and toxicity in the body. I find it very relaxing as well.

Acupuncture works in a similar fashion, but with the use of very fine needles – which I have to tell you are not painful!

Homeopathy. The concept of this therapy is that substances that cause particular symptoms in healthy people, such as raw onions causing sore, tearful eyes, can be used in extreme dilution to treat illnesses which cause the same symptoms. In this example, extract of raw onion could be used, extremely diluted, as an ingredient in a remedy to treat colds, flu, or other illnesses that produce the same symptoms.

The next case study is a bit different because it involves a dog! I've chosen this case because sceptics usually raise the possibility that autosuggestion or the placebo effect is the reason an alternative therapy is successful. You can find contact details for Cheryl Seers, the healer referred to in the following account, in the appendix.

Case study: The Power of You through alternative healing

Benson, a golden retriever, was two and a half years old when he first started to suffer extreme irritation and itchy patches on his skin. This was diagnosed as atopic dermatitis caused by dust mite faeces. His subsequent scratching resulted in large bald patches, and nothing that the vets recommended, including steroids, could alleviate his suffering. In fact, his condition got worse and he developed extreme alopecia. It got so bad that his owners considered putting him down to end his torment.

They were then recommended Cheryl Seers, a vet, healer and homeopath. She treated him with pure aloe vera to relieve his skin condition and put him on a daily dose of natrum mur, a homeopathic remedy. Within weeks his condition improved and now he has fully recovered. Needless to say, Cheryl is Benson's very best friend!

HERBAL REMEDIES AND SUPPLEMENTS

There has been a remarkable growth in the last few years in the use of vitamins and supplements, herbal remedies and tissue salts. A range of completely natural products – such as aloe vera, the sap of a cactus containing vitamin E, which is beneficial for skin problems – is now available at health shops. Herbal remedies were the traditional form of medicine in most cultures long before the first aspirin came to the market. They have proven their efficiency at healing, but in recent years they have been overshadowed by the growth of the drug industry and are now battling to hold their own in the market-place. There is a threat that the drug companies will take them over and the smaller companies with the experts who specialise in these remedies will be lost. There are those that fear that pharmaceutical organisations may suppress remedies that compete with their own chemically based products. If you feel strongly about this, as with any health issue, look for support and campaign groups and add your voice.

Which herbal or supplementary remedy do you need?

With the astounding choice of supplements and remedies now available, you need to turn to a professional and an expert for advice. There are two I can recommend: in the UK I go to Neal's Yard Remedies in Neal's Yard, Covent Garden, London, where a team of trained herbalists are ready to help you – or visit their website. In South Africa you will find Margaret Roberts, one of the world's leading experts on the growing and use of herbs and tissue salts. Her books (see appendix for details) will give great advice and recommendations on use.

Always buy your herbal remedies from a qualified herbalist. Take particular care if you are elderly or pregnant and never give a remedy to a child without getting expert advice. Ask the herbalist's advice and tell them of any pharmaceutical drugs you are taking.

'When you fight for your rights of choice you are empowered.'

HOW TO USE COMPLEMENTARY HEALING

When would you use a natural remedy or therapy instead of those offered by the health service? My advice would be to use complementary products and therapies rather than alternative ones. Complementary products can be used alongside any medication or treatments you are receiving from the health service whereas alternative therapies and treatments are intended as a replacement. With complementary therapies you can get the best of both worlds. If you need an operation to remove a tumour, have that operation. But use natural healing to release and heal the underlying problem in order to prevent a reoccurrence. Otherwise your treatment will simply be a sticking plaster that cures the short-term problem but doesn't do anything to heal the root cause – the holistic disharmony that sits underneath. If your energies are blocked by stress and underlying anxiety, any therapy that unblocks the natural energy flow will be beneficial, for example acupuncture, massage, reflexology, spiritual or Reiki energy healing.

'Empower yourself by caring for your body.'

Who do you use?

Complementary healing is an area of health care that has little or no regulation. Therefore, I recommend that you follow a recommendation by someone you know. If the first therapy or practitioner doesn't suit you, either because you don't feel comfortable with it or you just don't like the person, try another rather than giving up on the entire spectrum of treatment. I have put the names and contact details of my favourite therapists on my website (see appendix). The web magazine *What Medicine* (www.whatmedicine.co.uk) is a great source of current information on therapies and supplements.

Prevention

Many therapies are good at keeping stress levels down and act as good preventive 'medicine'. I have a massage every week and a reflexology session once a month to release any tensions in my body, especially when I am spending hours on my laptop. Apart from any other benefit, I love the experience of being pampered, of someone doing something lovely for me! This self-nurturing is a perfect balance to any work where you give out a lot of time and energy for others. Always keep in mind the need to nurture your body – you probably overwork it, stress it, ignore it, feed it with delicious but unhealthy food, and generally take it for granted. Use any treatment or activity that makes you feel good and uplifts your spirits to help bring a balance into your life. Work and play, work and rest, work and regenerate.

Body spirit

Your body has an elemental energy – I call it the spirit of your body. This spirit is naturally a positive and light energy, but when it has been misused in any way, its natural harmony is disturbed. This affects your physical body, often with disease or sickness.

Since you are a combination of emotions, soul, mind, physical body and bodily spirit, each aspect will affect the others. You may well have experienced this interaction when you get stressed. A period of anxiety during which your mind repeats negative thoughts will create disharmony, which will in turn become physical discomfort such as a headache or indigestion. Over time your heart and other organs can also be affected. So you need to respect your body and its spirit in order to keep it well and vital. As we have already seen, good eating habits, plenty of sleep and so on are important, but you should also show respect to your spirit – the elemental aspect of your body. This next meditation will give you the opportunity to express this care and also to bring love and harmony to all your personal aspects.

Meditation to heal your body and spirit

You can use this healing meditation on yourself or you can guide a friend or family member through it. If you are doing it for yourself, you will need a full-length mirror. Sit in front of the mirror.

✧ Close your eyes, let go your frown, drop your shoulders and breathe deeply four times. As you breathe out, let go of your worries and tension.

✧ Visualise a ring of pink light around you. See a blue light around the room.

✧ The most powerful energy for healing is love. Focus on your heart chakra, the energy centre in the middle of your chest. Touch it with your hand to establish the link.

✧ Imagine there are doors opening in your chest. This reflects your intention to open yourself to love – to enable you to give and to receive love.

✧ Open your eyes. See the mirrored reflection of your body – let this symbolise the spirit of your body. Sense beams of love leaving your heart centre and flowing towards your spirit.

✧ Speak to your body's spirit now. 'Thank you for enduring the misuse over the years, I appreciate your support and endurance. I release all tension caused by worry and fear, I release pain and tension. I love my body and care for its wellbeing.'

✧ Send love and healing to any part of your body that is
  suffering.

Through this investigation of health issues we have seen
that your actions, attitudes and approaches can give you back
a sense of personal responsibility and control, even when
you are ill. By making informed choices you can feel less
dominated and controlled by the 'experts'. Let's now apply
this principle to healing the environment and the world at
large.

SIX

Your Power to Heal Others and Your Environment

In this chapter I want to bring your attention to the problems we face with our environment. I also want to explore what we can do as individuals to make a difference, to live with respect for the Earth and to understand better the real essence and the spiritual aspect of nature and our planet. I will outline my perceptions of the elemental kingdom that inhabits and shares our world and show you how we can work with it to improve the state of our environment. I will also look at how even the smallest changes in our way of life can be significant in helping the recovery of our world and the healing of the damage that has been inflicted on it. This is an opportunity to bring your personal power into action.

'Through our will to change the world we can step into action, and action is hugely empowering for us as individuals and for all we hold precious.'

Since the beginning of the Industrial Revolution in the eighteenth century we have been abusing our environment. Chemicals and waste have been sluiced into our rivers and seas and the air choked with toxic fumes and smoke. In the last century we found an even more dangerous emission with which to desecrate the atmosphere – CO_2.

THE DAMAGE

The list of the damage we have done to our planet is endless. Let's just remind ourselves of some of the worst examples:

Rainforest destruction. One and a half acres of rainforest are lost every second, with tragic consequences for us all. This whole-sale destruction has serious implications for our weather patterns and is one of the major causes of global warming.

Extinction of animal species. Thanks largely to habitat loss, hunting and pollution, half the world's mammal species are declining in population and more than a third probably face extinction.

Poisoning rivers. Rivers, wells, seas and oceans have all been polluted by major disasters, chemical leakage, sewage and careless management. Already one person in five has no access to safe drinking water.

Atmospheric pollution. Many countries have managed to cut down their air pollution from factories and car emissions, but there is a long way to go and developing countries are struggling with this issue.

Overfishing. Large fishing boats, with good refrigeration capabilities, larger nets and large-scale fishing operations, have affected any number of species of fish including herring, cod and anchovy.

Declining natural resources. We have consumed large quantities of the Earth's natural resources, such as coal, oil, gas, wood and minerals of all kinds. We are using up 30 per cent more natural resources than the planet can replenish each year. This means we are selfishly living for ourselves, with no thought or consideration for our children or their children.

'When we harm our planet we harm ourselves,
when we nurture our planet we nurture ourselves.'

ENVIRONMENTAL DISASTERS

If the situation wasn't bad enough, there have also been major setbacks caused by specific man-made disasters. Here are just two of the hundreds of major environmental disasters we have created, with dire consequences for humanity, animals and plant life.

Chernobyl: Russian nuclear power plant explosion. In 1986 an explosion occurred in a nuclear reactor at Chernobyl in the Ukraine. It is estimated that up to seven million people were affected by radiation, and an area with a radius of 30 kilometres around the site has since been permanently evacuated as the land will be radioactive for hundreds of years. There are thousands of deaths still from cancer caused by radiation and it is estimated that over four million people live on contaminated ground.

Alaska: Exxon Valdez oil spill. This is just one of many major oil spills that have contaminated our seas and beaches and killed marine life. When the tanker *Exxon Valdez* collided with a reef in Prince William Sound in Alaska in 1989, the escaped oil polluted 1,900 kilometres of coastline and killed approximately 250,000 seabirds, 2,800 otters, 250 bald eagles and 22 killer whales. The chemicals used in the clean-up caused even more devastation to the birds than the oil itself.

Since I started writing this book, we have seen the world's worst environmental disaster, the Bay of Mexico oil rig explosion, and the resulting oil spill that has affected wildlife and the livelihoods of thousands. It throws up the question, why do we rely so much on oil that we put ourselves and our environment at such risk? Isn't it time we found a solution for this?

It is our individual need, demand and desire for the world's resources that has driven us towards the state of the environment we experience today. When we collectively decide that this is unacceptable, when we choose to live peacefully, when we choose to live more simply, when we choose to live harmlessly within our environment, respecting all life, then we will find answers and solutions. If you as an individual set an intention that this is what will happen, then gradually things will change. In the meantime, there are things you can do on a daily basis that will make you feel empowered rather than weakened by the situation we have created. You can do your bit to change the world step by step, so that gradually we will improve our environment and return all our world to its natural and beautiful state.

'When we make changes to our lifestyle that help the environment we become empowered.'

WHAT YOU CAN DO TO HEAL THE ENVIRONMENT

This is a subject that could fill an entire book! In fact, there are many articles, websites and books filled with information and statistics about the subject, so I just want to give you a taste here. Rather than spend too much time beating ourselves up, wracking ourselves with guilt and looking to who we can blame, I think we should focus on *action*. Although the situation and the future look dire, I am an optimist and I believe we have the intelligence, the imagination and the ability to find alternative power and effective ways to feed ourselves without destroying the planet.

The question is, do we have the *will*? Nothing works or changes without intention, and unless we as individuals and our governments choose to change, we will continue to lurch forward to self-destruction. Do you personally hold the intention to change your relationship with the environment, nature and our planet? I suggest you write down your overall intention now in your journal. As with any resolution, it can be your focus point and the beginning of change. Then you can begin to think out and choose your own action plan.

The following case study is drawn from a letter written by my colleague Dr Cary Rasof, who helps villagers in Zambia on behalf of our charity Hearts and Hands for Africa.

Case study: The power of recycling

The children collected all the trash in the compound, carried it to the school area and made a mountain of it. We then looked at it and did the needful. Nothing is valueless. There is nothing that is without some merit. So we took the plastic bags and cleaned them collectively. The kids love to clean. They adore it. We then dried the bags and took corn sacks, opened them and sewed them into the configuration of a mattress. Next we stuffed the mattress with all the bags and sewed it up again. Then the kids chose a grandmother in the compound who was poor and living on the ground. They brought the mattress to her and she was in seventh heaven.

They liked this so much that the next day they made another and brought it to another grandmother. Her house was so dilapidated and filthy that the following day they cleaned it out, swept and reorganised everything. Then they placed the mattress on the clean ground, fixed her door and washed her clothes before returning to school. There they took gum wrappers and made ornaments for the school, we took the *gitenge material the people wear around themselves and cut it into ceiling coverings displaying the colourful African designs and motifs. We then took all the rags from the garbage and made a carpet for the floor of the school. We won't have desks and chairs like other places. Then there is the garden that is happening with all the kids participating. And the playground . . . It's unreal. You must see it. You must see what can be created with the mind and will.*

YOUR PERSONAL ACTION PLAN

So let's now start putting together your action plan for living in an improved relationship with your environment. Remember, this is your plan, so it's up to you to choose what you put into that plan. I am just going to give you some suggestions.

Recycling waste. Take advantage of any recycling facilities in your community. If there are none, do your own where possible – many large supermarkets have recycling bins for all varieties of household waste. Separate out bottles, cans and paper. If you have a garden, compost your uncooked vegetable waste. Some councils have schemes to collect and recycle this for you, some offer free composters. Check with your local council.

By recycling used materials into new products we reduce:

✧ consumption of new materials

✧ energy usage

✧ air pollution (from incineration)

✧ water pollution (from landfill).

There are also considerable energy savings:

✧ Aluminium – 95%

✧ Cardboard – 24%

✧ Glass – 5 to 30%

✧ Paper – 70%

✧ Steel – 60%

The savings of recycling over new production are impressive. For example, aluminium recycling requires only 5 per cent of the energy and produces only 5 per cent of the carbon dioxide emissions compared to primary production and 70 per cent less energy is required to recycle paper than making it from raw materials. Recycling one plastic bottle gives enough energy to power a 60 watt light bulb for three hours, one recycled tin can gives power for a TV for three hours and one recycled glass bottle gives computer power for 25 minutes.

Clothes. The Salvation Army is one of many charities that collect and redistribute unwanted clothes. You can find bins for clothes in most districts, often in town centre car parks. I have a policy that I try to keep – though not always successfully, I admit – which is to turn out an item of clothing every time I buy something new.

Furniture. The Furniture Reuse Network includes 400 charitable organisations that collect furniture and household goods and sell them to people on low incomes. See www.frn.org.uk.

Light bulbs. Saving energy also saves money for you – an energy-efficient light bulb will save you up to £10 per year.

Unwanted possessions. Clear out your loft and find a new home for items you no longer have any use for. This helps reduce the effects of our 'throwaway culture'. Virtually every high street has a charity shop, or utilise FreeCycle (www.freecycle.org.uk), an international recycling organisation which has groups in most countries. On their website you can post requests for items you want and offer things you want to get rid of. It's a wonderful way to keep goods out of landfill and extend their use where they are needed.

If you want to recoup some money, use eBay or car boot sales. A friend of mine raised over a thousand pounds from her 'bits and pieces' when she needed funds to pay for a trip to Sri Lanka. Her determination to sell everything was particularly driven by the needs of the children at the orphanage she planned to visit as a volunteer. If you don't do it for yourself, do it for a good cause.

Your car. When you next need a new car, pick one that is eco-friendly, with low CO_2 emissions and low fuel consumption. The websites whatgreencar.com, www.green-car-guide.com and thegreencar.co.uk may be a helpful start.

Recycled products. There are many companies that specialise in products made from recycled materials. www.recycled products.org.uk has an amazing list, from bathroom fittings to decking.

Water. Take showers rather than baths. Install a water tub to collect rain water for the garden. You can install a 'Hippo' or save-a-flush bag for your toilet cistern and save up to three litres of water every flush.

Electricity. Currently our electricity is largely produced from fossil fuels or by nuclear plants that create toxic waste. Therefore the less electricity we use, the less impact we have on the environment and natural resources. Every little counts: lights, televisions, radios, cool wash washing machines, minimum use of tumble driers and so on. Other power-saving projects, such as insulating your loft and walls, will also help.

It has taken some time to get roof solar panel initiatives into full swing in the UK. I installed some for my office a few years back, but they weren't very efficient. I believe the new generation of systems are hugely improved; economically, though, it hasn't worked well in the UK and until recently there has been little incentive from the government. Germany, on the other hand, is the leading user of solar power in the world. Its 130,000 users can sell unused power to their local utilities and they are subsidised by the government. You might look for any opportunities to install solar panels or campaign for further support from the government for this power source.

Investments. If you have investments through shares, bonds or funds, then choose those that are in companies with green policies. There are plenty of reports on green shares in the financial sections of newspapers and on the web. I suggest you read *Green Money* by Sarah Pennells (see appendix), as she has thoroughly investigated this quite complex subject and gives plenty of good advice about where to put your money to the best advantage – that is, with companies and banks that run their businesses ethically and are helpful rather than harmful to the environment.

Children. You can help the future by educating any children in your family as to why we recycle, why we turn off lights, etc. *The Everything Kids Environment Book* by Sheri Amsel (see appendix) is a good introduction to the subject for children.

Action groups. When you want to influence change, you can be more effective if you add your passion and energy to a group. So join websites and action groups. These typically either lobby for change or are more practical in their efforts for the environment, for example by cleaning waterways such as canals and ponds, restoring country paths and tracks, or monitoring rare and threatened birds.

Petition. Write letters to your local council or Member of Parliament to support any law or project that will help the environment.

Charities. There are many charities that help the environment. Just as a few examples, the World Wildlife Fund does great work to save threatened species; Greenpeace campaigns to protect animals and the environment; Friends of the Earth seeks to solve environmental problems; Trees for Cities is responsible for planting and protecting trees; Stop Climate Chaos Coalition is a group of over 11 million supporters whose intention is to urge the UK government to bring in practical action to support climate change and Climate

Concern helps people understand the risks and dangers of carbon emissions.

Case study: The Power of You with initiative

I was sitting drinking coffee with friends at Johannesburg airport when a white-haired man came up to me and asked me if I lived in Bath. I said no, but added that I lived nearby. 'Oh,' he said, 'I saw your Bath Travel document case.' He went on to introduce himself as Julian Kotze and explained that he and his friend in Bath worked together to run a charity – RagBagSA. Julian and his wife work in the travel business, and they and their customers around the world collect children's clothing and hotel and airline giveaway toiletries for crèches, nurseries, day care centres and orphanages looking after HIV-infected children in South Africa. 'We recycle what people normally throw away to great use where it's needed the most,' he explained.

I rang Sandra, his friend in Bath, on my return and we found we had a lot in common. Apart from running charities we are all healers too. Sandra told me she had met Julian when he was her tour organiser on a holiday in South Africa. She had seen how little the children had, and had started this project with him after she retired. Since then she has collected children's clothes from an ever-growing group of donors in the UK, who themselves feel good about making the effort to make a difference. She says the charity has been a complete success for both the givers and the receivers – and she feels useful too in her retirement, a time when many people feel disempowered, that they are no longer needed. Her project is a great example of the power of initiative and action, showing how small acts can come together to create something bigger.

Any actions you take, no matter how small they seem, will give you the satisfaction that you are influencing the future of our planet. If we all do our bit we can make a huge difference.

'Small changes can make a big difference.'

SIGNS OF HOPE

There is no doubt that the Earth is warming and it is cause for great alarm. We should be concerned; after all, this is our legacy for our children. Kaia, aged eight, gave this response to my question, 'Why should we save the planet?'

> *'God created a beautiful planet and we need to learn how to take care of it and respect it. We must remember how to look after animals the way we would like to be looked after, as they are living creatures too. If we recycle and switch off lights it will help to stop the world from getting hotter. It is all really important because if the world just shrivels up — where will we all live?'*

Well spoken, Kaia — too true.

But there are signs that things are changing. Despite the loss of species through the development of rural areas throughout the world, anthropologists and naturalists are discovering new species and there has been some resurgence of those thought to be extinct. One scientist is recorded as declaring that there are hundreds of thousands of species on Earth still to be discovered — anywhere up to 100 million! Recently six thousand Irrawaddy dolphins, a species previously thought to be extinct, were seen in the sea near Bangladesh; while in Vietnam the Laotian rock rat and the saola, a cross between a deer and a cow, were discovered for the first time. Believe it or not, some anthropologists are still holding out hope that they will find the mythical yeti, although so far they have had only footprints and glimpses.

'Hope is the positive energy that leads to a better future.'

Although we may not be able to reverse climatic change, we can certainly change the cleanliness of the atmosphere, our countryside, our oceans and rivers. We can stop hunting and killing endangered animals, we can preserve the forests and respect the planet. We can petition for governments to bring in laws to enforce this. In April 2010, following campaigns and encouragement from environmental groups, a feed-in tariff for solar power and other green renewable energy was established in the UK, so that anyone who creates renewable energy, whether through wind farms or solar panel projects, will be paid above market rates. This is just the sort of change we should encourage.

Already there are signs that changes are taking place due to new laws, public consciousness and public care. In the UK there are no more pea soup smogs in London, fish are now seen in the lower reaches of the Thames and species such as otters are once again living in our rivers. In the USA the populations of endangered species such as bald eagles, wolves and grizzly bears have rebounded. New cars now use unleaded fuel, and more and more green options are available everywhere. In other words we are becoming green conscious. So let's keep a positive view on these situations. Do what you can, where and when you can, and step back only when you have no control whatsoever.

We will now take a closer look at some specific areas where we can help to make changes, starting with our urban environment.

IMPROVING URBAN LIVING

Generally speaking, our countryside still holds the positive and uplifting vibrations of nature, and most villages still hold a strong sense of community spirit. In our cities and towns, and even in large villages, life can be more challenging. The energy of a city is significantly different from that of the country and I particularly feel the change as I drive into the centre of London.

I was brought up in London and love the city, and I get a real buzz when I visit. However, after a few days I start to yearn for the peace of the countryside. When you are in a crowded place you will be affected at one level or another by the energies of those around you. You will feel the adrenaline that pulses through the vast numbers of people focused on work, achievement and reaching goals. You will feel the frustration of static traffic and travel delays. Although you can become stressed anywhere, there is more chance that you will feel the effects in city life and a city-based workplace. Life tends to be faster and more pressurised, more competitive and more expensive, while living conditions and travel are more challenging. You are also more likely to come across street crime in a city than in a country lane, so you need to be more aware, more careful of your safety.

You will need to focus deliberately and with a strong intention on releasing stress, frustration and anger – use the exercises given in the earlier chapters to ensure that your own energy is kept clear and calm. You can also use the various protection processes we have looked at to protect your energies whenever you go into a crowded place, so as to ensure that you are not adversely affected by the worries and concerns of those around you.

Let's now consider how we can improve our living conditions wherever we live, but especially in urban areas.

CONCRETE

The bane of modern living is concrete. It is everywhere. It is the energetic antithesis of nature. Thousands of houses throughout our towns and cities were built before the advent of the car and therefore are without garages or even hard standing for parking. As a result, owners have concreted their front gardens and turned them into parking spaces. Problem solved. In some areas, however, this has seriously affected the water table, while heavy rainfall causes the drains to overflow and flood because the concrete is unable to absorb the water.

What's more, in summer paved gardens absorb heat during the day; when this rises as it is released at night it affects the inside temperature of houses, so more and more people are resorting to air conditioners with the atmospheric pollution they produce. Above all else, the loss of gardens destroys the natural habitat of birds and insects, while plants no longer do their invaluable work of cleansing airborne pollutants and toxins.

'Wherever you can, take personal responsibility for your environment.'

WATERWAYS

In the past, many urban rivers, streams and canals were used as rubbish dumps. They have thus become overgrown, misused and ignored. Do you have any waterways near you? Are they kept clean and open? Moving water is a great source of positive energy for a city, as are gardens, parks, squares – and even recreation grounds, as long as their surfaces are made from permeable materials. They also offer a great natural habitat for wildlife.

WHAT YOU CAN DO TO IMPROVE THE URBAN ENVIRONMENT

There a number of practical ways in which you can counter these threats to our urban environment. If you need a parking space at the front of your home, use a permeable surface rather than concrete. Gravel allows water to drain away and won't hold the heat like concrete. The Royal Society for the Protection of Birds (RSPB) recommends cellular paving – recycled plastic 'honeycomb' matrix cells filled with gravel or recycled glass that make a good, strong parking area. The Royal Horticultural Society and RSPB websites both have plenty of helpful information. Keep as much space as possible free for planting. Encourage wildlife into your garden. Feed birds and put nesting boxes in shrubs and trees.

If you are fit and have free time, you could help any local projects to clear waterways. For example, the River Brent is due for a major facelift, while many of London's rivers that were once covered up, forced underground and paved over have been opened up through local authority initiatives. Canals throughout the country have been cleaned and brought back into use for recreation purposes. See your local paper and Citizens Advice Bureau for local projects needing volunteers.

Overleaf are a few ways to live in a city without adding any more pollution than necessary and while protecting yourself from the negativity of crowded streets.

Exercise: Are you in balance?

Urban living can throw you out of balance. So check yourself – are you in harmony with yourself and your surroundings, or do you need to find ways you can become calmer and more relaxed?

Draw two columns in your journal. On one side write down everything that you do, eat or experience that makes you feel uplifted and excited. What thrills you? What gets your adrenaline flowing? On the other side write all that calms you, relaxes you and brings you back into yourself. Use this list to see whether your life is in balance. How much time do you give to each side? Are you giving yourself enough relaxing and calming experiences?

We can take a few tips from the Japanese, most of whom live in crowded cities:

Bicycle. Use bicycles wherever you can and petition for more designated lanes and safe parking for bikes. You gain a health benefit from the exercise, while your frustration decreases as you skip the jams, and your travelling costs are lower. Obviously, cycling creates few emissions and is therefore better for the atmosphere. You may find a respiratory mask or charcoal-impregnated scarf useful to protect you from the traffic fumes – there are a number of options available on the internet.

Car. There are a number of good cases for a small and eco-friendly car for city use: lower emissions, lower tax, easier parking and no congestion charge. Oh yes, and less guilt!

Bus or train. Use local transport, which is usually good and cheap in towns. I lived in Hong Kong without my own car for a few years and there the local transport is amazing, with trams, buses and the metro as cheap options. And as a bonus, public transport saves you the cost and frustration of parking, which is horrendous in London, with cameras everywhere to catch errant parkers.

Parks. There are places of peace and quiet in most of our cities. Take advantage of them whenever you can, for their energy is extremely beneficial to you. Apart from the pleasure of walking through them on a sunny day, the plants give out beautiful energies that will uplift you and help you to release stress. I will expand on this aspect in the next section on the power of nature. Harass your local authority if your local parks are neglected.

Yoga. You can create your own special space and allow your own inner peace. I have found yoga a wonderful way to release the stress from my body and it gives my mind quiet time too. If it doesn't suit you, find something else that gives you a sense of peace, whether it be music, reading or just quiet contemplation alone. You need to feel you are in control of your life, and this can be harder in the city. You need to be the one dictating that there is balance in your life, with time for yourself and time to be centred away from the adrenaline rush and the fast lane.

If urban life destroys your sense of calm, here is an exercise to bring your focus to your needs.

Meditation to create your own inner peace

For your self-empowerment you need to be in control of a sense of balance in your life.

Balance
Find time for the fast lane and time for stillness,
Find time to socialise and time to dream,
Find time for steel and glass and time for plants and water,
Find time for music, phones and chatter and time for peace.

You are the only one who will bring about this balance – if you don't you will burn up and burn out. To help you gain a sense of peace, this meditation is designed to bring you back into balance and into your quiet and loving centre.

✧ Find a quiet space, turn off your phone.

✧ Flex your feet and stretch your arms and hands. Drop your shoulders and release your frown.

✧ See yourself as a great tree. See your roots entering the Earth, growing down deep through the many layers of the Earth's surface, through layers of rock, of crystal, through underground streams, deeper and deeper.

✧ Surround yourself with the violet flame of protection.

✧ Visualise yourself sitting by a camp fire out in the country-side. You are alone, but you are aware of a circle of friends and companions holding an outer circle around you. They are there to protect you and ensure you are not disturbed in any way. The moon is up and the stars are out.

✧ The fire in front of you is burning brightly and you stare into the flames. The light of the flames reflects your inner light – like you it flares up from time to time and then settles to a beautiful shimmering, flickering flame.

✧ Below the flames the logs settle and glow a deep red. They radiate gentle, relaxing warmth. Your limbs feel heavy and your body lets go any tension.

✧ As thoughts come into your mind, accept them. If they are persistent, ask them to enter the flames of the fire. Let the fire absorb all irritating, worrying and intrusive thoughts and transform them into a flare of light.

✧ Sense the mirror of the flame within yourself now. Know that within you burns a fire that brings force and strength when needed and yet can gently flicker when it's time for rest. Connect to your inner flame as it shimmers quietly within you, as your body, mind and spirit allow time for recovery and peace.

✧ Listen to your breathing. Let it be deep and slow as your body joins your inner spirit in relaxing and letting go tensions and stress. Focus on your shoulders and neck and see the muscles and tendons unwind. Your shoulder blades drop as you become more peaceful.

✧ Continue with your deep breathing and continue to welcome any thoughts into your inner flame. You are at peace and you are resting, and all is well.

✧ Stay by the fire as long as you wish. When you are ready to return, gently move your fingers and toes, hands and feet and gradually come back.

Take time with this meditation and use it anytime you feel stressed, anxious or overwhelmed.

We move our focus now from our social environment to look at how you can manage to keep yourself strong when you are in an area of conflict.

'Through love and respect we can change so much in our world.'

CONFLICT

If your home has been in a location of conflict of some kind – perhaps war, terrorism or rioting – the spirit of the area will need healing in the same way that a person who has lived through a bad experience does. A friend of mine who lives in Athens rang me last year when her city was badly affected by riots, mainly involving students, one of whom was shot by the police. The riots caused untold damage and misery to shop owners and businesses in the city and affected everyone who lived or worked there. Scared and angry, they asked why they were the victims of other people's frustration and anger – what had it to do with them? It's a question we often ask when we get caught up in any form of aggression. But we are all connected, and when part of our society is suffering – or, as in this case, angry – then we are all affected, some more directly than others.

We need to be concerned and feel responsible in some way. I cannot sit in my house in the New Forest and claim no connection to under-educated, disaffected, angry young men rioting in a housing estate in Liverpool or Athens, mad because they feel left out of society with no access to the group financial and happiness pie. They are part of the bigger me. Similarly, if a young Islamic fanatic shows his hatred for Western culture and thinking by setting off a bomb in the middle of London, killing and maiming, we are all affected. Let's see what we can do to assist the energy and spirit of the places where these disturbed energies damage everyone's peace and harmony.

WHAT YOU CAN DO TO HEAL CONFLICT

When my friend called me from Athens we both used one of our most powerful tools – distant healing. It's possible by this means to send healing to areas of disharmony and conflict within our society; we can help to disperse the negative thought forms that hover above, holding the fear, anger and judgement that are created by such outbursts of civil disruption. The next meditation not only sends healing to the discord, it clears the negative energy blocks and focuses love upon the hearts of all those involved; upon their anger, frustration, loss and fear. If you find it difficult to visualise, just say the words and know your good intention is helping to make this happen.

Meditation to heal any community, village, town or city that has suffered from discord, conflict or generally needs its spirit lifting

✧ Close your eyes, ground yourself and relax your shoulders.

✧ Visualise yourself surrounded by a violet flame, a burning purple fire. This will protect and clear your energy.

✧ Visualise a pink ring of love around the place that you wish to help.

✧ Open your heart with loving intention to assist all those involved, whether they seem the perpetrators or the sufferers of discord and conflict.

✧ Say out loud or in your heart, 'I send love and compassion to all concerned, I send love and healing to the environment and all those who have suffered through this conflict.' Visualise rays of love travelling from your heart to the area and the people concerned.

✧ Send love and healing to the atmosphere, the air and the sky above the problem area. Know that the love will dissolve and transform the negative thought forms that hang overhead.

✧ Say, 'I transform all the anger, despair, fear and hate and turn it back to love, positivity and joy. May this place be blessed with peace and harmony through the hearts of all who live, work or visit and may the environment be cleansed and free of all negative thoughts, attitudes and actions.'

✧ Draw the symbol below in the air three times and visualise it hovering overhead. Given to me by my spirit guides, the symbol represents the eternal flame of light that clears away darkness. It will emphasise and send the message of peace and harmony.

Now I will explain a little more how important it is that we acknowledge all aspects of our natural world, and that we don't throw it out of balance through disrespect and mismanagement.

CONNECTING TO THE POWER OF NATURE

Now I am going to step out of the box. I am going to share with you both the obvious and the hidden powers of nature – trees, plants, water. We will look at how you can connect to the incredible powerhouse of energy that is the spirit of our planet.

For the last two years I have given an extended workshop at Shambala, a Buddhist retreat centre which sits beside the River Findhorn on the Moray Firth in Scotland. It is the most delightful place to step away from life and take time to heal and recuperate. It enjoys a microclimate which is affected by the warmth of the Gulf Stream, so it is mild throughout the year. And the light up there is very special. It is also part of the Findhorn Community, founded by Eileen and Peter Caddy in the early sixties and now the most famous and established spiritual community in Britain.

After running a local hotel for some years, the Caddys and their friend Dorothy McLean found themselves homeless with three children to support, so they moved to a caravan park near the coast at Findhorn. Peter planted a vegetable garden in the park grounds and the magical light of Findhorn was ignited when Eileen started to communicate with the spiritual overseers of the plants in the garden. Through their guidance the garden's herbs, flowers and vegetables started to flourish in an extraordinary way; its famous cabbages weighed in at 40lb!

The Caddys' success drew attention from around the world and over the years the foundation flourished, developing into the spiritual educational centre and eco-village of today. It is now particularly famous for putting green policies into action. In its earlier days it was considered a fringe, New Age centre for hippies and scorned by mainstream society, but now it is respected as a centre of expertise for ecological and environmentally friendly living. And the community still grows amazing vegetables that I can personally recommend!

THE SPIRITUAL ASPECT OF PLANTS

As Eileen Caddy discovered more than forty years ago, every plant and every tree has an aspect of spirit that governs and guides its growth and wellbeing. This spiritual energy force ensures that every plant follows its blueprint of being – rather like our DNA. Whereas we each hold an individual genetic code, plants have a group code that determines their size, colour and so on, so that all daisies, for example, will look alike. By listening to and respecting the spiritual plant guides, Peter and Eileen were able to allow their plants to grow to their full potential. This mirrors our own quest to be as great as we can be, and to be who we are without interference from the old experiences, fears and phobias that limit us.

'Your love and respect for nature has a powerful and positive impact on the environment.'

Every culture has experienced these spiritual plant overseers, although many have either forgotten them or – thanks to the materialistic and scientifically driven mindset in which we live today – simply pushed them aside. These nature spirits have an angelic quality to them. They don't have the free will that humans enjoy, but they are a loving energy programmed with their particular role of performance. Those that look after flowers and plants are often referred to as devas. I am fortunate enough to have a developed sense of inner sight, which enables me to see, as if on an inner video screen, past lives and spiritual energies, and I see these natural energy beings in various forms – very often as beings of swirling light and colour. However, there are some people – lucky things – who can actually see them with their naked eye!

One of those people was R. Ogilvie Crombie, a Scottish academic nicknamed Roc. A wonderful elderly gentleman from Edinburgh, he had some incredible experiences in the city's Botanic Gardens where he met with a nature spirit in the form of a faun – a creature with the appearance of a man from the waist up and the lower body of a goat. In his delightful book *The Gentleman and the Faun* (see appendix for details), Crombie describes the magical conversations he had with the faun, who introduced him to the amazing Pan. The spirit of Pan, which appeared to him as a larger and more powerful version of the faun, represents, governs and rules the elemental, vegetable and mineral kingdoms. He is an extraordinary force of intelligence, light and compassion.

Pan explained that we humans cause suffering to the spirits of plants and consequently to our natural world. Every time we cut down trees, clear vegetation or reroute rivers we create natural chaos. Many spirit beings are torn apart and disconnected from their source of being, leaving them without purpose. Through this suffering they begin to shed their positive vibrations and, instead of the gentle loving energies that we feel when we walk through parks and gardens, they radiate a lower, negative vibration. These lower energies are often identified as bad spirits or even evil spirits – although this is a misnomer, for they are actually damaged spirits, damaged by us.

'Every aspect of your wellbeing and inner balance
is improved when you connect to nature.'

ELEMENTALS

Apart from spirits that have the purpose of guiding the well-being and growth of plants, there are a number of other energies that are related to the Earth. These Earthbound spirits are referred to as elementals and they all have positive purposes for the land or the plant kingdom. Elves, fairies and fauns are just different forms of these spiritual beings, and they are not only the subjects of myths and fairy tales but are in fact elemental forces of energy that exist in the hidden dimensions of spirit.

Elemental spirits work with the four elements of water, fire, air and earth. They help to clear pollution and atmospheric toxicity, but if their existence is ignored they lose their potency. When volunteer groups cleared the canals and rivers in England, the energy of these spirits was uplifted and revitalised. If those involved had actually spoken to the spirits and asked for their help and – even better – apologised on behalf of humankind for the filth and neglect that their domain had suffered, they would have found their work easier as the energies would have lifted immediately.

WHAT YOU CAN DO TO HELP RESTORE NATURE

First, show respect for nature spirits and for nature itself. Take quiet time in your garden, park or open countryside to speak to these spiritual beings. Ask them for forgiveness on behalf of humankind for the dreadful things we have done to the environment. If you wish to connect to a specific nature spirit like Pan or the Deva of Roses, then put your-self in protection and call their name. Allow your imagination to materialise an image of the spirit in your mind. We all see the nature spirits differently depending on our reception and experience.

When you need to cut down a tree or move a plant, just take a moment to connect to the spirit of that plant and acknowledge it. Tell it what is happening. When we recently cut down a number of fir trees, I asked the spirits that worked with the trees to move to fruit trees we had recently planted. I thanked the devas of the trees, the genetic spirits, for their work in bringing the trees to maturity, and said goodbye to them.

You even can send love and healing to assist the life forms of animals, birds and insects affected by the devastation of earthquakes, fires or volcanoes, asking the spiritual beings to help you. This can be done with the help of newspaper articles showing pictures or maps of the problem area. Draw the peace and harmony symbol (see page 220) three times in the air and place your hand onto the paper. In this way you can send healing to people, situations or countries.

And if you get the opportunity to visit a sacred site, visualise a white light filling the place and see it as a cleansing energy force, clearing away any negative influences that may have affected the energy vibration. When I travel, I use Ripple's Clearing and Cleansing plant extract spray to quickly clear any space that I feel may need uplifting.

Whatever you are doing, see yourself as a micro-organism of a larger group energy, like a body, that includes Mother Earth (or Gaia – the Ancient Greek word for Earth used nowadays to mean the spirit of Earth). Your intentions and the way you treat yourself radiate out to and connect with the greater body. By looking after your own body in ways like the following you can also positively influence the health of the greater body:

✧ Detoxify and clear away the toxins in your body left by tobacco, alcohol and chemicals in food and water.

✧ Exercise and take in fresh air.

✧ Eat fresh, healthy food.

✧ Grow your own vegetables and eat organic where you can.

✧ Meditate on the holistic nature of your own being – the harmonics and empathy of body, mind and spirit of your energy being and that of the spirit of Mother Earth.

Through the next meditation, you will learn to focus on the connection that you have with our planet, see yourself as the microcosm of the macrocosm and understand that everything that you do, that you experience, that you think and intend will affect the planet. As you become more empowered, more in the state of love, more joyous, so you are doing your bit to change the world.

Meditation to heal the planet

In performing this meditation, it may help to have a map of the world or a globe with you to give you a focus for your loving energies.

✧ In a quiet place, relax. Close your eyes and drop your shoulders.

✧ Ground and protect yourself.

✧ Imagine you are holding the world in your hands or place your hands on the map. Feel the love flowing from your heart and your hands to fill the planet.

✧ Know that every plant, every animal and every rock is connecting with your heart now. You are sending out love and they are sending back love – a beautiful circuit of light spins between the planet and you. It is continuous and constant, a shimmering spiral of love light bringing and giving strength and love.

✧ Allow this love light to move to every part of your body that needs healing.

✧ Know that every disturbed nature spirit, every polluted waterway, every broken energy line, every traumatised sacred site, is filled with this love.

✧ All is loved and all is healed. Send love and healing to Pan and his spirits and thank them for all they do to keep nature alive.

As we have learnt, then, we have many hidden helpers that can assist us in our quest to improve the state of our environment. As we have also seen, we can do much ourselves, both through care and attention and through action. We can take action ourselves, we can gather others together and act as a group, or we can encourage those in authority to act to bring about change.

HELPING EACH OTHER – COMMUNITY CONSCIOUSNESS

Helping anyone at any time has a ripple effect that influences everyone. Every kind action will make at least one person feel better, will make them feel cared for and loved, and that person in turn will then ripple out their own uplifted vibrations. This principle of the Ripple Effect is explained more fully in my book of the same name. Voluntary work, acts of kindness to friends, family or strangers, all help tremendously.

Many of the effects of negative forces trouble us on a daily basis, whether it be the overwhelming bureaucracy of the benefits office, the bank's arrogance and mistakes, the government's idiocy in taking us to war, the neighbours playing their music too loud, or the fumes in the atmosphere. But all of these can be faced more easily when you share or get help from someone else. We all have different outlooks, skills and gifts to offer each other. The challenges of form filling, the difficulties posed by computers or legal jargon – all may be easy for one and a nightmare for another. The more we help each other, the happier we will be as a community and a nation.

SPEAKING UP FOR OTHERS

Earlier in this book we looked at the Power of You to take responsibility for yourself. We now focus on how you can express this responsibility in the bigger picture of life. You can take your ability to speak up and use it to stand up to even the most overpowering and controlling of forces. The largest organisations and the law can be changed if you decide to make an effort to do so and are prepared to go the distance, digging deep for fortitude and endurance.

If you have seen injustice that you feel needs reparation, then act and make it your responsibility. In your role of taking control and make choices, why not choose to act and put your contribution into the energy of change? You will be well rewarded – for the success you achieve, even if it takes years, will make you strong and truly empowered. If you are troubled by the injustices of the world you might like to join one of the many action groups who specialise in finding justice, for example INNOCENT, a group who fight miscarriages of justice.

Remember the parable of David and Goliath from the Bible, where a simple boy killed the giant Goliath with a sling and shot. He dared to do it. Dare to take on your own project and fight the cause yourself. Here are a few examples of modern-day Davids:

✧ Actress Joanna Lumley campaigned to win for Gurkhas equal rights with the rest of the British Army. Through her endeavours a policy to deny the men British residency was overturned in Parliament. Thanks to a previous campaign, they were also given equal pension rights.

✧ Soldiers injured in combat will now receive more compensation due to the campaigning efforts of Diane Dernie, the mother of a 23-year-old paratrooper who was severely injured when blown up by a bomb in Afghanistan.

✧ In 1952 Rosa Parkes refused to give up her seat on a bus to a white person in the US state of Alabama. This hugely symbolic act of defiance helped to bring an end to segregation and legal racial discrimination in the American South.

Well done to them for their courage – they are great examples of personal power in action.

'You can change the world little by little.'

Case study: The Power of You to change the world

Greg Mortenson was a regular young guy. His great love was rock climbing and mountaineering, and when he wasn't pursuing his dream to climb the world's highest peaks he worked as a hospital nurse. In 1993, when descending from an attempt on Pakistan's K2 mountain, he found himself exhausted and lost on the lower slopes. He stumbled into a village where he was nursed back to health by some of the poorest people in the world. He saw the young girls of the village taking lessons outdoors and discovered the village elders' dream that one day their children would have a purpose-built school. Since then he has dedicated his life to raising funds and organising the building of girls' schools in the remote and inhospitable terrain of northern Pakistan and Afghanistan.

Through his efforts − and the hard work of the local villagers − hundreds of schools have since been built. His is a mission of empowerment and peace − empowering the girls with education, empowering the villagers to build their own schools, empowering those that give donations and empowering himself through his amazing life's work. He has brought opposing cultures together and brings peace through education and literacy.

You can find information about Greg's inspiring books in the appendix.

'If you passionately believe in a cause or are incensed by an injustice, then SPEAK UP AND ACT.'

VOLUNTEERING AND COMMUNITY ACTION

Throughout this chapter I have referred to activities and groups that have already been set up to help others and the environment, and details of these are given in the appendix. However, there will be many other initiatives and volunteer organisations in your area that offer help and support to those in need – for example, driving the elderly, sick and handicapped to hospital appointments, teaching children to read, working with Scout and Guide groups and other youth organisations, visiting the elderly, providing relief for carers and so on. If there is nothing that meets the needs you see and the skills you can offer, then set up your own group. All these are positive experiences, all ways to make you feel good about yourself and make other people's lives better too – a true win–win situation.

'Helping others lifts them and fulfils you.'

There is no doubt that giving and sharing bring huge personal rewards. The most fulfilled and satisfied person I know is my friend Douglas Maclagan, the founder of the Child Welfare Scheme. He lives and works in Nepal where he has set up village support groups, clinics and hostels for street children. His life is rich and interesting – and challenging, of course – and his work brings him immeasurable pleasure. And it shows!

As Douglas and thousands of others have found, helping others and offering your time and care has a beneficial effect on both parties. A government-run national survey of volunteers came up with the following results about the reasons why those interviewed did voluntary work. The figure shows the percentage importance weighting given to each point.

I really enjoy it	70
I get satisfaction from seeing the results	68
It gives me a sense of personal achievement	49
I meet people and make friends	49
It gives me a chance to do things I'm good at	35
It broadens my experience of life	38
It gets me out of myself	31
It gives me more confidence	31
It makes me a less selfish person	30
It makes me feel needed	27
It gives me the chance to learn new skills	26
It makes me feel less stressed	19
It improves my physical health	18
It gives me a position in the community	15
It gives me the chance to improve my employment prospects	12
It gives me the chance to get a recognised qualification	6

Case study: The Power of You in the community

My charity, Hearts and Hands for Africa, focuses on help-ing orphaned children in Zambia. My project partner Dr Cary Rasof and I both had a great fear that our patronage and charity would disempower both the children and the women who care for them, so we evolved a way that we could help them and their communities without taking away their own power – which would in fact empower them and offer them an opportunity to sustain themselves without aid.

We give micro-loans to the carers, often grandmothers, to enable them to build up their own businesses – farming, trading, sewing, etc. – so as to create the funds to feed their children and help the many orphans who cannot attend school due to lack of money for books and shoes. To join the loan project the women have two entry fees: to build a fuel conservation stove – a covered stove made of mud bricks, to be constructed by themselves and their neighbours – and to plant fruit trees in their village. This way both the community and the environment benefit. So far over a thousand trees have been planted and hundreds of children have returned to school, all through the efforts of the women and their communities.

We celebrate this as a win for the donors, as we are empowered by giving; a win for the children who are fed and have an education; a win for the environment; a win for the children's communities, who share in the giving and receiving; and a massive win for the women who are empowered by their success and sense of achievement.

YOUNG PEOPLE IN THE COMMUNITY

Young people in particular can be affected by crowded living conditions and poor job prospects. Although most young people are confident, sure of themselves and of who they are, there are also many who feel insecure and look for some form of identity outside of themselves, associating in cliques and gangs – especially in areas where unemployment is prevalent and people generally feel a sense of hopelessness. This can lead to antisocial behaviour and violence. Everyone in the community then suffers, including the teenagers themselves.

WHAT YOU CAN DO TO HEAL DAMAGED COMMUNITIES

Many of the actions needed to revitalise housing communities and regenerate a sense of spirit, care and trust between neighbours and to give some sense of purpose and identity back to the children are out of our hands and in the control of government and the inhabitants of the estates themselves. However, there are things we can do.

Petition

Write letters to MPs and take an interest in the problems the people living in these situations face. I have given a number of workshops in Liverpool and many of those attending have been funded by EU grants specifically given to help volunteers who go into these estates (for example Toxteth, which was pulled apart by riots in the eighties), and offer a number of therapies. Many of the residents are suffering from all manner of physical and mental problems and these schemes run by volunteers have proved very successful, not least in that they make people feel they are of value and that their problems are acknowledged. They also help to break down prejudice and the judgement that surrounds anyone living an underprivileged, impoverished lifestyle.

Volunteering

There are numerous websites that offer information on charities and schemes that need volunteers. One of these is the British Trust for Conservation Volunteers (BTCV), an international voluntary organisation that supports conservation initiatives around the world. If you don't have a computer, you can find information on local groups at your Citizens

Advice Bureau or your library, or you can contact your local radio station or newspaper.

One of Britain's biggest voluntary groups is Community Service Volunteers. CSV is Britain's leading volunteer and training charity, with over 150,000 volunteers; they help and touch the lives of over a million people every year. They run numerous projects and opportunities for volunteers of all ages and pride themselves on never turning away anyone. Their voluntary schemes include gap year volunteering, retired and senior volunteering, mentoring of young people and youth volunteering, while their Action Earth scheme gives funds and support to help you set up your own local environmental project. Currently there are 200 such projects that they have helped get off the ground.

Case study: The Power of You through volunteering

Jimmy lives in central Scotland and his life was quite a struggle, with battles with drugs and alcohol. He tried many different jobs without success – he felt very uncomfortable working for others and making money for another person to enjoy. Eventually he found his niche by working and volunteering with young people who had also been struggling – many of whom suffered from mental health issues and had experienced battles with addiction too. He now runs a day centre where he encourages young people to enjoy gardening and learn to cook. He is helping them to feel worthwhile again.

Find the voluntary group that suits you best in your area. Giving to others, sharing your skills or your time is rewarding, fulfilling and empowering, so you will probably find that you gain as much as you give. As we have seen, my husband pulled himself out of post-retirement depression by joining Dormen (Dorset Business Mentoring), a voluntary mentoring organisation to help small business get started. If your life is full and you have no time to spare, all these charities need donations. If you are suffering from low self-esteem, volunteer work will help you revitalise your own sense of self-value.

Speak up

If you have any opportunity to speak up, either socially with friends or to a wider audience, on the subject of tolerance, acceptance, encouragement for those who are in living in difficult circumstances, then do so. It's so easy for society to look down on and judge people living in these situations. We can make change by sharing our loving aspect and passing it on whenever we get the chance.

Distant healing and meditation

Quantum physics describes nature as a unified field in which every tiny particle of matter exerts an influence on every other particle. Therefore we can radiate great power through our thoughts and we can use this energy to bring about change. This is the way distant healing works – healers send visualisations of their patient recovering, accompanied by love. Love energy is the energy with the strongest, most positive and highest vibration; with this combination of thought power and love, we help to raise the energetic vibration in specific situations from negative to positive. Through this method, meditation and distant healing groups have had some amazing effects on lowering crime figures.

There are various methods you can use, but here is one way it can work.

Meditation to lower crime rates and discord in a community

✧ Gather a group of any number of people, but the larger the better as the results grow exponentially with the size of the group.

✧ Focus on one location. This might be a town, village or housing development.

✧ Meditate using your intention through visualisation to lower the level of crime in that location. Picture a bar chart and visualise the bars getting lower and lower as the recorded crime drops. You could even create a chart that shows the current figures dropping and let everyone focus on that – this will help those that find visualising difficult.

✧ Hold this visualisation for a few moments.

✧ Then focus on your heart centre, the energy centre in the middle of your chest which is your doorway to love. See and sense it opening.

✧ Know, see and sense love flowing from your heart directly to the community you wish to heal. See and sense everyone living together in harmony. You only need to hold this for a few minutes.

That's all there is to it! Easy and effective!

Case study: Helping the community

Every Christmas May and Kingsley get ready for their Christmas lunch like millions of others around the country. The difference is that they are cooking it not just for themselves but for those who have no permanent home and who live on the streets. They have been doing this for years, since their own son and daughter grew up and left home. They say it is by far the most fulfilling way they could spend their Christmas, though needless to say they fall back in exhaustion with a large drink by late afternoon! They say that the smiles and appreciation from their fellow diners makes it all worth while.

If this appeals to you, find out more about festive volunteering by visiting the websites listed in the volunteering section of the appendix.

Throughout this book I have highlighted things that are wrong or upsetting, and which deplete our individual control and power. There is tendency to expect 'them', the government or the authorities, to 'do something about it' – this is the downside of having a welfare state. By taking that attitude we miss the opportunity to take responsibility for local situations, to make contributions on a one-to-one basis. We miss the 'we all help each other', co-operative way of living which is much more rewarding at a personal level. However, we can have the best of both worlds, for there is a case for devolution – the passing of certain responsibilities and authority down to the local community in order to let the people make choices at grassroots level about issues that affect them personally.

In the meantime we do what we can by setting up local playgroups, shopping rotas for the elderly or litter-clearing teams, establishing a Neighbourhood Watch for security and watching out for those that slip through the benefit net. That way we bring the great human values of justice, self-responsibility, kindness, compassion and love to our society – and when we do it for others we do it for ourselves. There can be nothing more empowering than that.

Having looked at the practical help we can give each other, I would like to finish this chapter by focusing on ways that we can use our mind energy to positive effect for the greater good of all. The combined energy of us all, the greater energy force that comes from all our thoughts, all our emotions, all our energy outflows, is called mass consciousness.

USING THE POWER OF THOUGHT TO HEAL MASS CONSCIOUSNESS

The energy of everything we think and say has to go somewhere; it can't disappear, although it can change form. All our thought energy and its accompanying emotions come together as one energy being – mass consciousness. This includes the accumulated thoughts of every family unit, village, city, county, tribe, race, creed and nation. We are all affected by the state of this mass consciousness and we all contribute to it.

In recent years a number of major disasters, both natural and man-made, have caused stress all over the globe. We have looked at some of these and at what you can do to help, but it's also useful to understand the impact they can have on the energy of mass consciousness. You may well have been affected by this energy. Imagine the impact on the atmosphere around our planet of all the fears, anxieties, remorse and anger that are swirling around us. Is it any wonder that you find it hard to rise above it some days? Is it any surprise that you sometimes feel heavy and disconsolate without any apparent reason?

Mass consciousness energy not only affects our feelings, it also affects our attitudes and the way we think. It is easier for us to be positive when the atmosphere around us is uplifted, joyous and positive. It would be hard to stand in the crowds at the World Cup in South Africa and not feel the joy. As the majority of a group change, so it is easier for us to change too.

On the negative side, this is the reason a good and kind man may get caught up with the energy of a riot and do things that he would never normally contemplate. On the positive side, this energy mass will affect our desire or reluctance to go to war. There were mass protests before the Iraq war in 2003 and since then public opinion has swayed even further from any prospect of conflict. We are aware of the problems with the environment and individuals all over the world are recycling and turning off lights. We are more compassionate – record sums are collected by charities and we gave over seven billion US dollars for the victims of the 2004 tsunami alone. In fact, I felt the effects of the heart opening that came with the outpouring of gifts and donations. It was great to see so many people caring for strangers, wanting to help and giving so generously – a true exhibition of our human spirit at its best. Every year in the UK we raise millions of pounds for Children in Need and Comic Relief for poor and disadvantaged people around the world.

All vibrations of energy have an impact. Energies spiral and move towards similar energies – they cluster together and create clouds. On one occasion I was running a group healing session with about eighty people outdoors in South Africa. As I led them to let go their fears and anxieties, I became aware of a vortex of spinning energy leaving the group, swirling past me and off into the atmosphere. I could feel the cobwebby sensation I sense whenever I connect to negative energy forms. Once the energies of love were called in as we opened our hearts, I felt a familiar 'whoosh' as these energies filled us and the atmosphere around us too.

Mass consciousness is affected by all the positive energies we radiate, our upbeat and happy thoughts – our love and kindness to family, friends and strangers, our moments of joy, our elation at our own success or that of our friends or favourite sports team, our celebrations on birthdays, anniversaries and national days. These have a huge impact on our world group energy; positive and uplifting energies transform the negative energies and disperse the clouds of doom and gloom. If we know that our thoughts and feelings can affect others, then we can use this to change world feeling.

'Everyone in the world is affected by every kind thought and kind action.'

WHAT YOU CAN DO TO HEAL MASS CONSCIOUSNESS

We radiate our sense of wellbeing and uplifted energies unconsciously and we will affect anyone we meet with these energies, but there are times when it is useful to intentionally direct positive vibrations towards someone else or towards a situation in the world. The moment you think kindly of someone, or adopt a caring, compassionate attitude, you are affecting not only that person but, in the bigger picture, the energy of all of us. When you work on your own healing and positive attitudes, you affect the mass consciousness and therefore everyone on Earth. You can also deliberately send positive vibrations to people, nations and the planet. In the next meditation our intention is to clear the negative thought forms that hover around us by using consideration and love.

'Share your love and good feelings with everyone and help uplift the world.'

Meditation to uplift mass consciousness

✧ Close your eyes, drop your shoulders and breathe in deeply four times.

✧ Surround yourself with the violet flame of protection.

✧ Focus on someone you love and see beams of love as pink streams of light flowing towards them now. See them surrounded by this love and caressed by tenderness.

✧ Now think of a situation in the world where there is suffering or conflict. See beams of your love leaving your heart and going straight to the heart of the problem. See the people recovering, see people laughing and sharing. See them dancing and celebrating together as the conflict is resolved, as the troubles end.

✧ Next direct your thoughts and focus on the clouds of darkness, the fears, guilt, shame and anger – the negativity of humanity – that hovers above us. Direct laser beams of loving energy from your heart centre to disperse these clouds.

✧ Know that these clouds of darkness are being dissolved by your love and sense of compassion for all of humanity, every child, every woman and every man on Earth.

So we leave this chapter, about helping other people and the environment, on a spiritual high note. In my final summary to this book we'll look at ways you can focus on your empowerment through mind, body and spirit. And in conclusion we shall bring the powers of strength, love and wisdom together to be the fullest force of your human spirit, the force that breaks all limits and allows you to be in the complete state of fulfilment and joy.

SEVEN

Strength, Love and Wisdom is the Power of You

As we have seen throughout this book, there are many challenges to your personal power and many ways you can flex your muscles and take on these challenges. In this final chapter I will summarise the practical ways that you can reinforce, protect and develop this aspect of you holistically, combining the perspectives and interconnecting forces of your mind, your body and your spirit to unleash the full force and Power of You. I will end this book with a reflection on the spiritual power you unleash when you combine the forces of will and love.

ACTIVATING YOUR PERSONAL POWER THROUGH BODY, MIND AND SPIRIT

Remember that the power of your will is always there. It may be hidden but it is most definitely there for you – waiting to be activated and utilised to ensure you have a full and joyful life. Through the holistic approach of the interaction and connection of all aspects of yourself you can access your personal power and activate it through your mental, physical and emotional aspects. Each aspect will affect the other. As your body becomes fitter so your spirits will lift, as you read an uplifting story so you become energised, and so on.

Let's remind ourselves of the ways that you can choose to develop your personal power, which is a combination of your courage to face challenges and fears; your inner strength to overcome them; and your determination to keep going and not to give up.

COURAGE – FACE YOUR FEARS

Mind. Overcome your fears by visualising yourself tackling them and winning. See yourself as the gentle warrior fighting for justice and fair play for yourself and others.

Body. Gently push yourself in training, raise your expectations of what you can achieve. Step forward rather than back. In your sporting endeavours, go the extra yard. If there is something you fear to do, be brave – have a go. Do the right thing. Act rather than passively watch or be the victim of injustice or bullying.

Spirit. Speak up when it would be easier to keep quiet. Stand up to the bully in the office. Let your goals and dreams drive you, rather than your fears.

STRENGTH – STAND STRONG, HEART OF OAK

Mind. Use affirmations to clear your mind of negativity and fill it with positive thoughts. 'I am like an oak tree, nothing can push me over', 'I am strong enough to take on all my challenges'.

Body. Through weight work, build up your core strength and your muscles. Visit the gym regularly to focus on your physical strength.

Spirit. Be firm, learn to say no when you have had enough. Use tough love with your family and friends, where you are strong for the greater good of the whole group. Speak up when others threaten to dominate you.

DETERMINATION – BOUNCE BACK, SHOW STOICISM, FORTITUDE, WILL POWER

Mind. Think positive even when the odds are against you. The greatest lessons come from failures. You can have another go when things go wrong or obstacles are put in your way. Visualise your goal and know you will meet it.

Body. Take up long-distance running and endurance sports. Reach the power to keep going no matter how difficult it may become.

Spirit. Cry, then wipe away your tears and have another go. You will never be beaten, no matter what comes at you. When you are discouraged, share your feelings with others and let their spirits uplift you.

Now add the power of love, because strength without love can be a brutal thing, love without strength is passive. When you combine the two you unleash the greatest force of the universe, the light of life, the joy of living.

LOVE – KINDNESS, COMPASSION, CARING, GENTLENESS

Mind. Think kindly of yourself and others, find ways to help whenever you can. See through people's faults and difficult behaviour and see their inner light. Use the power of your mind to visualise yourself and others happy and peaceful. Forgive and let go negative thoughts.

Body. Love and care for your body by resting it when it needs rest, feeding it with good and nutritious food, listening to it when it complains that mind and spirit are out of balance. Kind actions show your love.

Spirit. Retain your perspective of benefit and care for yourself, others and the planet in everything you do. Sing and dance when you can to show your love of life. Focus on gratitude and the wonderful aspects of yourself and your life. Share your love with everyone through kindness. Open your heart and share compassion with the less fortunate.

'You have the incredible gift of free will, that is the foundation of your power base.'

YOUR EMPOWERMENT CHECK LIST

Here is a list you can put on your fridge. It is your guide for empowerment.

✧ *Make it work for you*. Change your work not for money but for fulfilment.

✧ *Say it how it is*. Tell your best friend, partner or family what you really feel, digging deep and baring your soul.

✧ *Pass it on.* Help others either through your work, by volunteering your time or sharing financially. There is absolutely nothing like the feeling when you have helped to empower someone or relieved their suffering in some way. *There is nothing more empowering for you than sharing and giving.* I guess you can see I really, really believe in this one!

✧ *Forgive and forget.* End feuds or avoidance of old friends or family. If you can't forgive, accept them for what they are.

✧ *Treat yourself.* Your own personal uplift – mine is to put on make-up, especially lipstick, every day, even when I am working at home.

✧ *Face the world.* Present your best face to the world! Taking care of your appearance is a big boost – especially for women.

✧ *Rave it and rage it.* Know it's OK to be angry, but don't upset others with it. Rage alone! Pump the pillow, scream it, write it and burn it.

✧ *Unfinished business.* Complete any healing process, give yourself time to get over the hurtful or harmful experience.

✧ *Face your fear.* You will always feel better when you have confronted your fears.

✧ *Work the body.* Many of us get a good vibe from exercise.

✧ *Open your heart.* Keep your heart open to receive and give love – love is the most empowering emotion you can live and work through.

✧ *Victim to victor.* The bully looks for the weakest victim. Do you attract negativity? Do you wear a sign saying 'Hit Me'? If so, pull it down. See yourself as the victor not the victim.

✧ *Feed your force.* Eat well. Find the food that suits you. Everyone's body needs a different regime; listen to your body and see which foods energise you and make you feel strong.

✧ *Personal strength equals personal responsibility.* Take your life in your own hands, feel and sense your own responsibility for all that happens, all the choices and all the outcomes of your life. You are in control.

✧ *Power in numbers.* Work with others to make change.

✧ *Nature will help.* Use the natural properties and energies of Spruce, Cedar and Pine essential oils, and Labradorite and Agate, Cinnabar, Jasper, Opal, Quartz and Ruby all of which have the energies that enhance inner strength and power.

✧ *Way to go.* Have an action plan of all the things you want to do, dream of doing, feel the need to do; which campaigns you want to join or start, new ventures for yourself, education and opportunities to expand your mind, charities you want to support with time or money, addictions to release, social events you wish to organise, goals for work and play.

YOUR PERSONAL POWER OF LOVE AND STRENGTH CREATING JOY

This brings me to our final meditation exercise to combine the aspects of strength and power with those of love and compassion. These inner forces are within us all and are traditionally expressed through the masculine energy of action and strength and the feminine energy of love and nurture. These masculine and feminine energies are within all of us, although depending on our sexual orientation we obviously have more of some than others. We need both to be physically active and to be true to ourselves, to be spiritually active, to overcome our fears and to allow ourselves to live life to its fullest. This union of strength and love triggers a sense of total expansion and allows you to experience the force of human spirit to its greatest potential, expressed through joy and ecstasy.

Feminine energy. Represented by heart energy, the chakra and energy centre located in the middle of your chest, feminine energy is love, compassion, tenderness, consideration, thoughtfulness, nurture, caring and creative. It is expressed in lives by our caring, loving ways with children, the elderly, the sick and animals. Its creative powers come through childbirth, art, music and design.

Masculine energy. The subject of this book, represented by solar energy, the sun energy of our solar plexus chakra above the navel, masculine energy is strength, courage, action, determination, grit, durability. It is expressed in our ability to stand up and fight for our rights and those of others, to be strong and courageous when challenged, to speak out with strength when bullied. It is the force we need to protect ourselves and our families, the ability to work and provide for ourselves and our loved ones.

Meditation for the union of strength and love

In this meditation your inner power of masculine energy, centred in your solar plexus, is represented by the sun, your feminine energy is the focus of your heart centre and your wisdom is your Higher Self, your Oversoul that collects the wisdom of all your lifetime experiences. I will lead you through this as I bring in the energies of universal solar energy and we together reconnect your will, your love and your wisdom.

✧ Close your eyes and relax. Drop your shoulders.

✧ I see you surrounded by a pink circle of love. Around your room is a blue circle of light that only love can enter.

✧ See yourself as a great tree with roots that grow deep into the ground beneath you. As your roots grow deeper and deeper you are strongly connected to the Earth and become stable and strong.

✧ Focus on your intention to express your personal power through love and wisdom.

✧ Touch your solar plexus with your right hand. This is your energy centre of strength, control and action. This energy force governs your self-esteem and identity. Visualise your solar energy as a disc of golden light, spinning in a perfect circle.

✧ I connect with the universal energies of the spiritual sun, the solar logos, and from this great sun bring down to you a beam of golden light.

✧ Let the force of the universal energy of strength combine with your golden orb. As the energies of these suns combine, you feel the force of your will, strength and courage magnify as your golden light gets brighter and brighter.

✧ Sense the force of your inner sun burn up and transform your self-doubts, your fears and anxieties, guilt and remorse. As the flames devour them your sun grows brighter and brighter. Your doubts become understanding, your fear turns into strength and guilt becomes self-appreciation.

✧ Allow the experiences of your past to become the wisdom you take forward.

✧ Touch your heart chakra in the centre of your chest with your left hand. This is the focus of all love you give and receive. See the doors of your heart open to receive unconditional love.

✧ My heart opens and touches your heart and universal love flows into your heart now.

✧ See this spinning into a swirling circle of pink light. Allow this energy of love to absorb all your grief and sadness, your sense of rejection and separation.

✧ As more and more love flows into your heart, see and sense this force of love transforming grief to delight, rejection to inclusion and a oneness with every living being. The light of your heart grows brighter and brighter as you become consumed by love.

✧ We bring the energies of your solar plexus, your inner sun, into full union now with the love in your heart. As the powerful forces of love and strength combine, you open to joy and ecstasy. Allow that joy to flow through your entire being. Surrender to the experience.

✧ We connect the power of strength, will and love to the higher wisdom of your higher and divine self. The force of your personal power is now complete – with this fusion of strength, love and wisdom flowing up and beyond you now to bridge the separation between you and the rest of the world.

✧ Beams of joy burst forth, penetrating and moving through the fears and doubts of humanity. You are now experiencing human spirit in its finest and most magnificent form. Your energies have no limitations. As you share them with the world you are now able to utilise your greatest potential, allowing you to fulfil and manifest all your hopes, dreams and visions.

The human spirit in its fullest, most positive power expresses itself through will, fortitude, determination, strength, generosity, compassion, sympathy, love, durability, tolerance, justice and wisdom. Your personal power is the experience of this spirit. When you are in your full power you will live your life to its fullest potential, bringing fulfilment, happiness and joy. Can you think of any better way to be?

Appendix

RECOMMENDED READING

Sheri Amsel, *The Everything Kids' Environment Book: Learn How You Can Help the Environment By Getting Involved at School, at Home, or at Play*. Adams Media Corporation, 2007

Marcia Angell, *The Truth About the Drug Companies*. Random House, 2005

Robert Canfield and Mark Victor Hansen, *Chicken Soup for the Soul*. Vermilion, 2000

Stephanie Cave, *What Your Doctor May Not Tell You about Children's Vaccinations*. Warner Books, 2001

Robert Ogilvie Crombie, *The Gentleman and the Faun: Encounters with Pan and the Elemental Kingdom*. Cygnus Books, 2009

Elizabeth Gilbert, *Eat Pray Love*. Bloomsbury Publishing, 2006. A woman's journey to finding herself and happiness through the gifts of Italy, India and Bali

Jo Griffin and Ivan Tyrell, *Freedom from Addiction*. HG Publishing, 2005. Helps you to understand why any pleasure-giving substance or pastime can become addictive

Robin Griffiths and William Houston, *Water: The Final Resource: How the Politics of Water Will Affect the World*. Harriman House Publishing, 2008

Patrick Holford, David Miller and Dr James Braly, *How to Quit without Feeling S**T*. Piatkus, 2008. Nutritional treatments to assist in ending addiction to caffeine, sugar, cigarettes, alcohol, illicit or prescription drugs

Anne Jones, *Heal Yourself: Simple Steps to Heal Your Emotions, Mind and Soul*. Piatkus, 2002

Anne Jones, *Healing Negative Energies: Simple Steps to Improve your Energy at Home and at Work*. Piatkus, 2002

Anne Jones, *The Ripple Effect: A Guide to Creating Your Own Spiritual Philosophy*. Piatkus, 2003

Anne Jones, *Opening Your Heart: How to Attract More Love into Your Life*. Piatkus, 2007

Anne Jones, *The Soul Connection: How to Access your Higher Powers and Discover Your True Self*. Piatkus, 2008

Jamie Khoo, *Call Me Paris*. Kechara Media & Publications, 2009: available from Kechara.com. A delightful, inspiring book to prove to any young person that following your spiritual path can be anything but limiting and boring

Gail Liberman and Alan Lavine, *Rags to Riches: Motivating Stories of How Ordinary People Achieved Extraordinary Wealth!* Dearborn Trade, US, 2000

Neil Z. Miller, *Vaccines: Are they Really Safe and Effective?* New Atlantean Press, 2003

Greg Mortenson, *Stones to Schools*. Penguin, 2010

Greg Mortenson and David Oliver Relin, *Three Cups of Tea*. Penguin, 2006. The story of Greg's determination and passion to help the children of the North East Frontier of Pakistan

Sarah Pennells, *Green Money: How to Save and Invest Ethically*. A & C Black, 2009

Michael J. Roads, *Talking with Nature – Journey into Nature*. New World Library, 2003

Margaret Roberts, *Tissue Salts for Healthy Living*. Jonathan Ball, 2009: available from www.margaretroberts.co.za

Joe Simpson, *Touching the Void*. Vintage, 1998. A story of courage and determination against enormous physical odds

Sharon Snir, *Looking for Lionel: How I Lost and Found My Mother through Dementia*. Allen & Unwin, 2010. A must read for anyone caring for someone with dementia or short-term memory loss

Sue Stone, *Love Life, Live Life*. Piatkus, 2010. Inspirational book that follows Sue's amazing experiences of the power of positive thinking

WEBSITES FOR SUPPORT AND ACTION

ENVIRONMENTAL ORGANISATIONS

Climate Concern: www.climate-concern.com
Campaigning for increasing understanding of the dangers of climate change and for encouraging energy savings

FreeCycle: www.freecycle.org.uk
An international recycling organisation

Friends of the Earth: www.foe.co.uk
Information and action on climate change

Furniture Reuse Network: www.frn.org.uk
400 organisations that collect furniture and household goods and sell to people on low incomes

www.greenfinder.co.uk
Has a large list of charities that help the environment

Greenpeace: www.greenpeace.org
An international organisation caring for the environment

www.recycledproducts.org.uk
A comprehensive list of products that are made from recycled materials

Stop Climate Chaos: www.stopclimatechaos.org
A charity caring and campaigning for the environment

Trees for Cities: www.treesforcities.org
Charity that plants trees in cities

Whatgreencar.com
www.green-car-guide.com
thegreencar.co.uk
Information on the environmental aspects of cars

WWF: wwf.panda.org
Supporting animals in danger of extinction

HEALTH AND ADDICTION

Action on Smoking and Health: www.ash.org.uk
Helping with cigarette addiction and health issues relating
to smoking

Alcoholics Anonymous: www.aa.org
Helping those suffering from alcohol addiction

www.directgov.uk
Holds a lot of information and help for both addiction
and those supporting an addict

www.gamcare.org.uk
An international list of support groups and manned
helplines, chat lines and counselling service for gambling
addicts

National Drugs Helpline: 0800 776600

www.patient.co.uk
A useful site filled with information about support and
help for many addictions

PEACE AND DEVELOPMENT

Campaign Against Arms Trade: www.caat.org.uk
Works for the reduction and ultimate abolition of the
international arms trade

The Child Welfare Scheme: www.cwsuk.org
An international development charity founded by Douglas
Maclagan, dedicated to supporting disadvantaged and
vulnerable children and young people in Nepal

International Alert: www.international-alert.org
Works around the world, both directly with people
affected by violent conflict and at government level, to
shape the building of sustainable peace

Landmine Action: www.landmineaction.org
An organisation that supports the clearing of land mines

RagBag: www.ragbagsa.org.uk
Recycling children's clothing for orphans in South Africa

THERAPISTS AND HEALERS

Stone Balancing: www.stonebalancing.com
Andrew Gray shows how stone balancing can calm the mind

www.breathingspacetherapies.com
Annie Lawler shares the techniques she used to heal
herself after stress burnout

Neal's Yard Remedies: www.nealsyardremedies.com
Expert herbalists

Ripple UK Ltd: www.make-ripples.com
A company founded by Anne Jones with aromatherapist

Debbie Mulkern, producing essential oil blends for healing and unique jewellery based on powerful ancient scared symbols

Cheryl Seers MVB, MRCBS, VET MSHOM:
www.hampshireholisticvet.co.uk
Offers homeopathy, acupuncture (both needles and laser), herbal remedies, Bach flower remedies, nutritional medicine

What Medicine: www.whatmedicine.co.uk
A magazine with a directory of therapists and alternative healing

www.health4humanity.org.in
To campaign for the support of herbalists and herbal medicine

VOLUNTEERING

British Trust for Conservation Volunteers: www.btcv.org
An international volunteer organisation helping conservation projects around the world

Community Service Volunteers: www.csv.org.uk
Britain's largest volunteer organisation, covering all aspects of voluntary work and training

www.volunteering.org.uk
For volunteering opportunities

You can also search online databases such as www.do-it.org.uk or www.timebank.org.uk

OTHER WEBSITES

www.achievezine.com
Inspirational video clips

INNOCENT: www.innocent.org.uk
A group who fight cases of miscarriages of justice

www.oneplace.direct.gov.uk
A very useful site for information on public services, your rights, how to report crimes, children's safety, help for carers, local environmental issues, schools and so on

www.webstudio13.com
Thirteen of the most inspiring YouTube videos

Dormen: www.dormen.org.uk
The Dorset Business Mentoring Programme (Dormen) provides one-to-one mentoring support for small businesses across Bournemouth, Dorset and Poole

ANNE JONES

ANNE JONES COLLECTION: WWW.ANNEJONES.ORG

Visit my website for a CD recording of the Power of You meditations. Other products and workshops that can help with the work in this book are: online healing videos, meditation CDs, my books, InnerSight Cards, Healing Symbol jewellery and information on my retreats, workshops and healing. All profits go to my charity, Hearts and Hands for Africa (see p. 264).

THE POWER OF YOU: WWW.THE-POWEROFYOU.COM

An opportunity to share your personal experiences of empowerment and inspiration. Visit my Power of You website for seminars, webinars and empowering true stories. The seminar series includes:

✦ The Power of You the Therapist

✦ The Power of You in Business

✦ The Power of You with Nature

✦ The Power of You to Conceive

For further details of workshops and a brochure call Brenda on 0771 075 3498.

Contact me: Anne Jones P.O. Box 7230, Burley, Hants. BH24 9EE, anne@annejones.org

You can follow my schedule on Twitter and Facebook – AnneJonesHealer

HEARTS AND HANDS FOR AFRICA: WWW.HEARTSANDHANDSFORAFRICA.COM

HELPING PEOPLE HELP THEMSELVES AND THEIR ENVIRONMENT

The profit from my books, workshops, healing sessions and product sales is donated to my charity Hearts and Hands for Africa, working in Zambia.

Our intention is to uplift those living at subsistence level and poverty in a way that empowers them rather doling out handouts and charity. We want to give back power to the vulnerable to make choices about their lives rather than to be caught in a constant struggle for survival.

Our first focus has been the women in rural areas who care for their own children and orphans. My partner in this project is Dr Cary Rasof, a medical doctor whose experience working in Rwanda and Angola has proved a huge asset. He is based an hour from Lusaka and spends most of the year working there setting up our projects which are driven from a micro-loan plan that fuels small enterprises and gives autonomy and sustainable support to the women.

To join the plan, the women and their communities are required to build fuel conservation stoves and plant fruit trees in their villages and compounds, helping to replace the many trees that have been destroyed in the past.

Self-sustaining projects affiliated to the Micro Loan Plan are Goats for Grannies, Kids Back to School, Nutrition for Aids and Community Schools.

The results have been heartwarming and beyond our dreams, and the enthusiasm of those participating in the giving and receiving is a lesson for us all as we see true empowerment in action.

UK Charity Registration No. 1122515
P.O. Box 7230, Burley, Hants. BH24 9EE

RIPPLE ENERGY THERAPY: WWW.MAKE-RIPPLES.COM

Ripple Oil blends for healing can be purchased from www.make-ripples.com.

These include Letting Go – to assist in cutting cords to past experiences and connections, Protection – to protect your energies from the influence of others, and Cleansing and Clearing – to clear your space of negative energies and atmospheres.

Index